AF314025

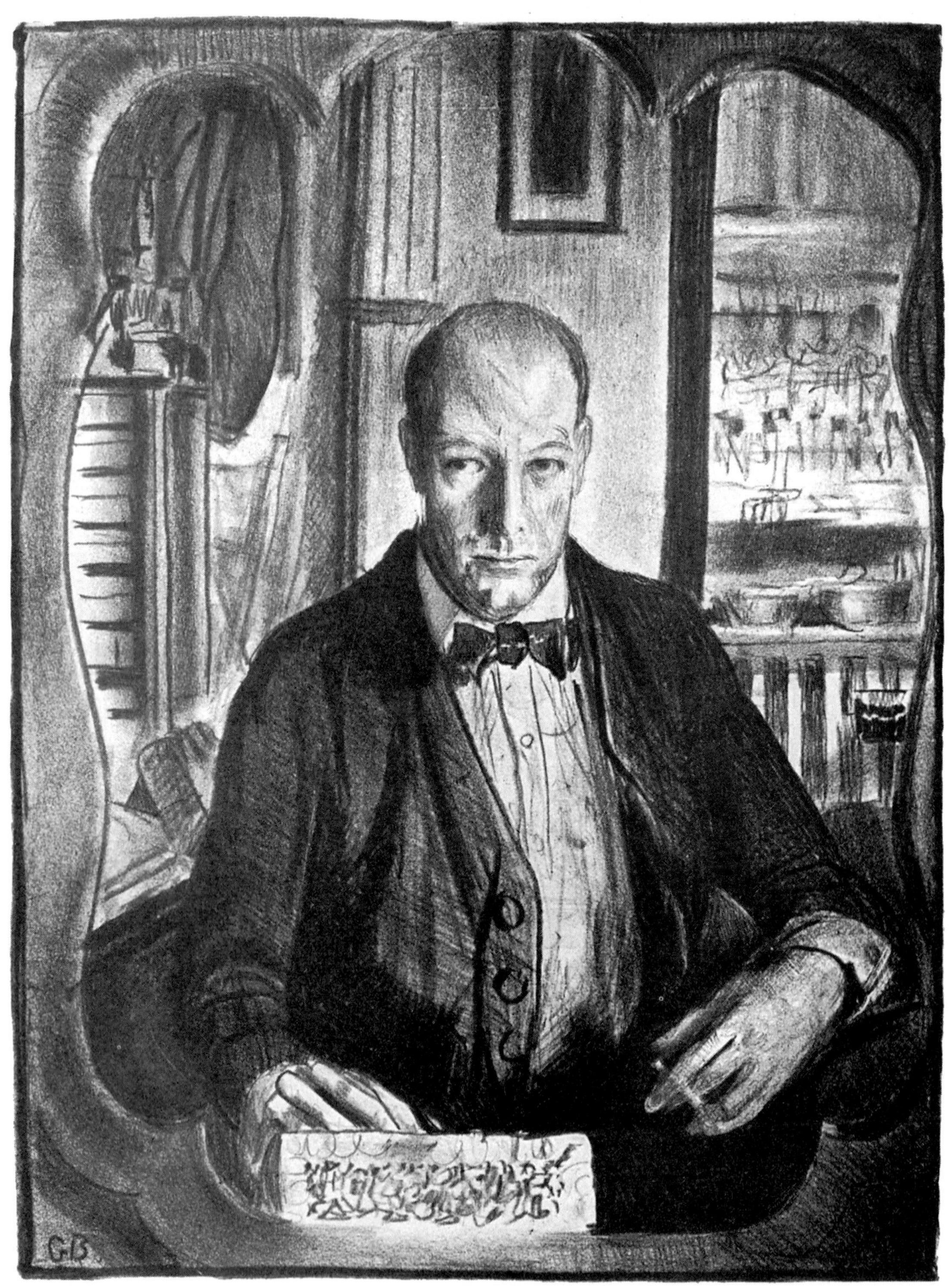

Self-portrait

THE VIBRANT METROPOLIS

88 Lithographs

GEORGE W. BELLOWS

Selected by
Carol Belanger Grafton

DOVER PUBLICATIONS, INC.
Mineola, New York

Copyright

Copyright © 2002 by Dover Publications, Inc.
All rights reserved under Pan American and International Copyright Conventions.

Bibliographical Note

The Vibrant Metropolis: 88 Lithographs is a new work, first published by Dover
Publications, Inc., in 2002.

Library of Congress Cataloging-in-Publication Data

Bellows, George, 1882–1925.
    The vibrant metropolis : 88 lithographs / George W. Bellows ; selected by Carol
Belanger Grafton.
       p. cm.
    ISBN 0-486-42304-2 (pbk.)
     1. Bellows, George, 1882–1925—Catalogs. I. Grafton, Carol Belanger. II. Title.

NE2312.B44 A4 2002

2002074188

Manufactured in the United States of America
Dover Publications, Inc., 31 East 2nd Street, Mineola, N.Y. 11501

INTRODUCTION

Born in Columbus, Ohio, painter and lithographer George W. Bellows (1882–1925) was one of America's most dynamic artists. An only child born to middle-aged parents, Bellows liked to draw, and spent many afternoons amusing himself with his own drawings and compositions. He contributed illustrations for his high school and city newspapers and was the leading cartoonist for his college yearbook. His devout Methodist parents sincerely hoped their only son would study for the ministry, and tried not to encourage his artistic pursuits. The young Bellows also excelled at sports, and played baseball and basketball at Ohio State University. At the end of his junior year, Bellows abandoned his dream of playing professional baseball to pursue a career in art in New York.

Noted for his portrayals of sports and action scenes—particularly his spirited boxing matches—Bellows came to New York City in 1904 to study with Robert Henri and John Sloan. Henri, his foremost teacher at the New York School of Art, was the principle leader of the Ashcan School (also known as The Eight), a group of realist painters that depicted the poor and the downtrodden in city life. It was here that Bellows found his artistic niche. By the age of twenty-seven, Bellows was elected an Associate of the National Academy of Design—the youngest member in the organization's history at the time. By the time he was thirty, he had become a full academician and was gaining a national reputation. He was one of the few among his contemporaries not to study abroad, and in fact, he never left American soil during his lifetime.

Bellows organized the 1913 New York Armory Show, to which he submitted fourteen of his own paintings. Interested in compositional order and balance from early on in his career, Bellows was a disciple of Jay Hambidge and his design theories of "dynamic symmetry," which proposed a strict set of formulas that based pictorial arrangement on a substructure of geometric shapes. Bellows also studied the paintings and prints of Goya and Daumier. He enjoyed watching crowds of everyday people in the street and attended prizefights at Tom Sharkey's, a popular entertainment bar in New York City. His paintings and lithographs reflect the exuberance of urban life, and he successfully captures a spectator's excitement for the moment.

In 1916 Bellows began to make lithographs. At first, he experimented with etchings, after admiring those created by his close friend John Sloan. An etching was drawn with a metal stylus through a film of wax onto a metal plate, after which acid was applied to finalize the design. However, Bellows soon found that the medium of lithography was better suited to him, since it was more direct and personal. For a lithograph, an artist drew directly on the printing stone with a rich crayon. Using broad, bold strokes and a masterful use of shade and light, Bellows brought an amazing vitality and energy to lithography. He bought his own press and pursued printmaking with his inimitable passion and fierce love of life. Between 1916 and 1925, he produced nearly 200 lithographic images, many of them black-and-white replicas of his paintings. He completed fifty-nine images within the year 1921 alone—a prolific effort testifying to his intense drive.

Like his paintings, Bellows' lithographs convey the sense of a pure American spirit. He possessed an unusual natural gift as an artist, and generally drew without models, accomplishing this with incredible ease. The only elements of research for his famous boxing scenes were based on his own visual memories, and his vast imagination filled in the physical details. He once reflected that he focused on the movement of his subject in depicting such themes as prizefights and street scenes, not on any particular facial expression. These sometimes-faceless subjects in dramatic settings charge his work with an enormous amount of energy and lend his characterizations a life of their own. His lithographs encompass a wide variety of subjects, ranging from urban genre scenes of the Ashcan School, to portraits of his wife and two daughters, to the violent atrocities of World War I.

An inventive painter, Bellows tried to capture the essence of America in the ordinary people and situations around him. Although the public considered his refreshing honesty and frankness brutal and coarse at times, critical acclaim followed quickly. Bellows elaborated on his earthy and forthright approach to art: "The ideal artist is he who knows everything, feels everything, experiences everything, and retains his experience in a spirit of wonder and feeds upon it with creative lust." He died prematurely at the age of forty-two, following emergency surgery for appendicitis.

CONTENTS

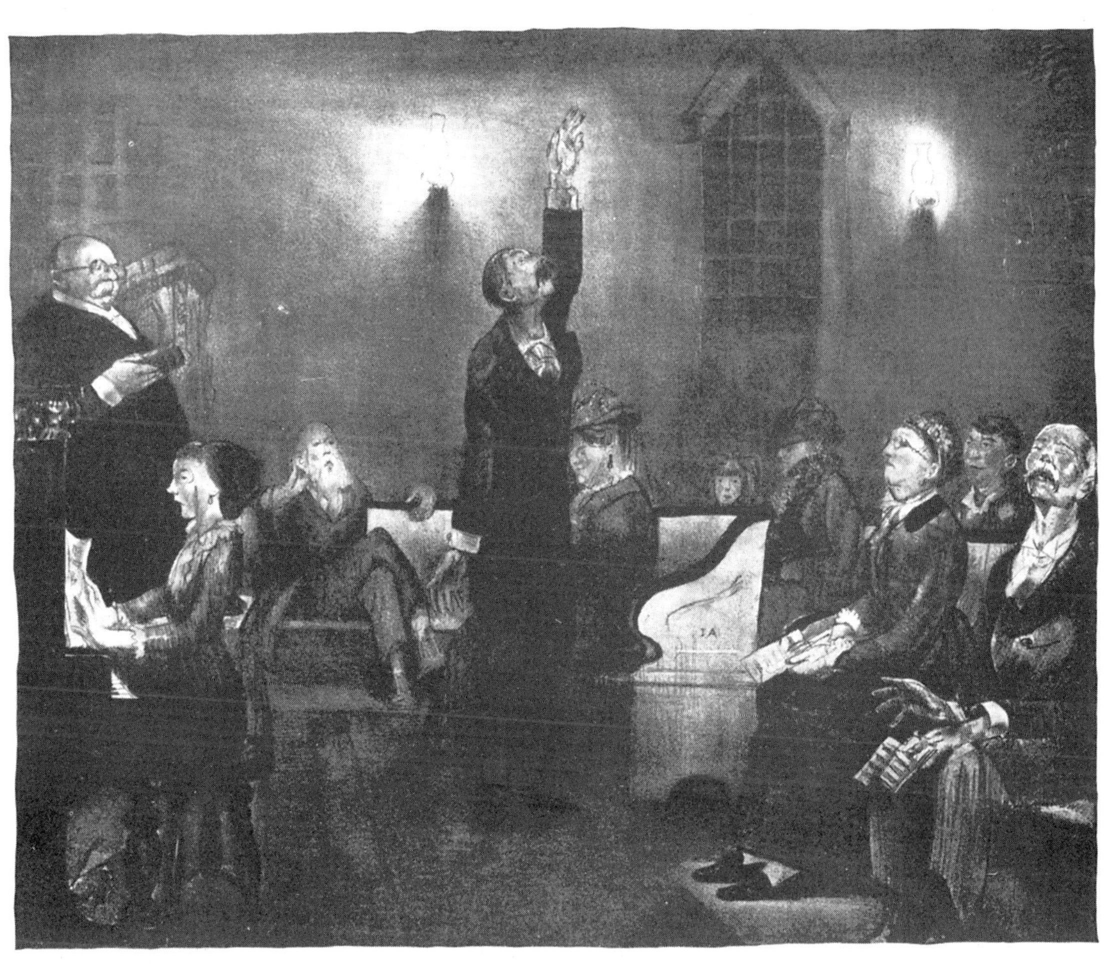

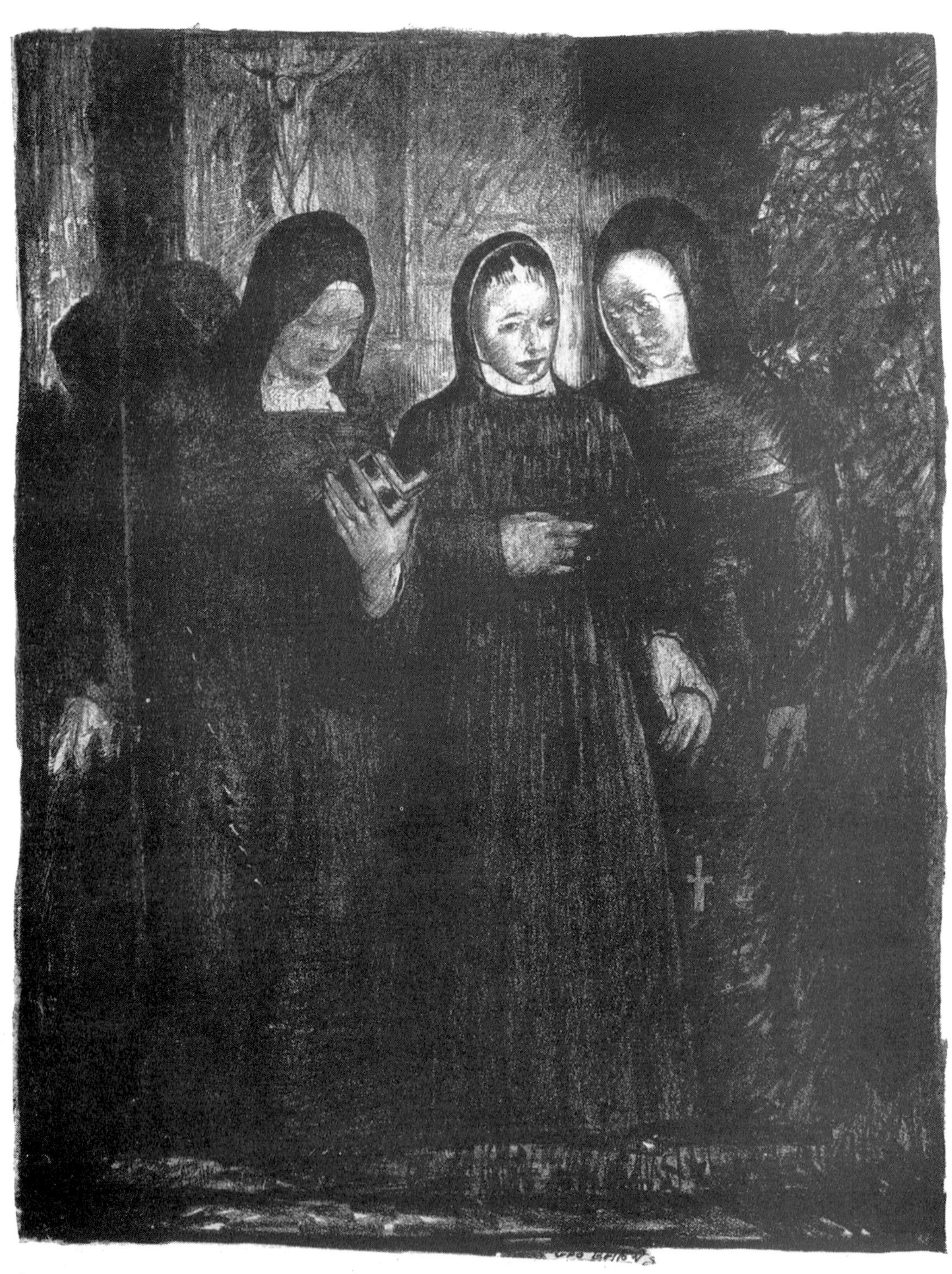

  The Novitiate

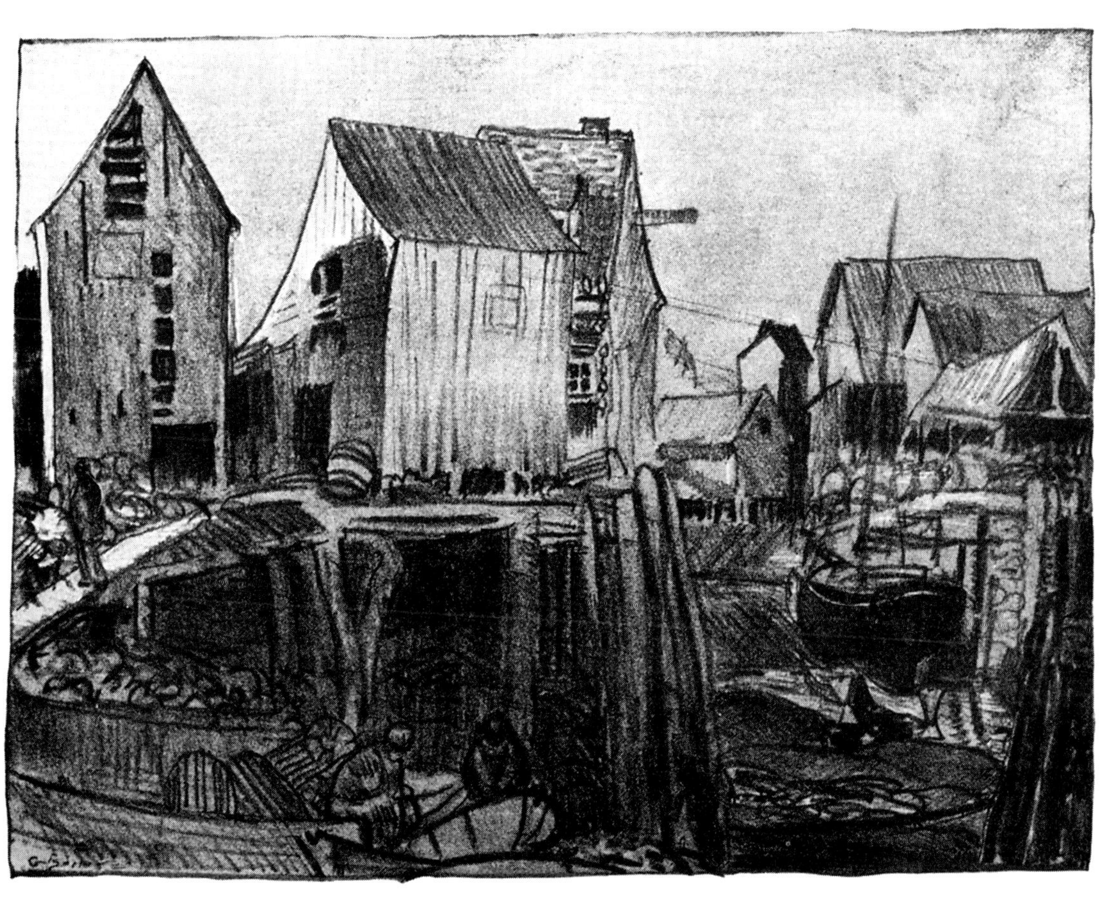

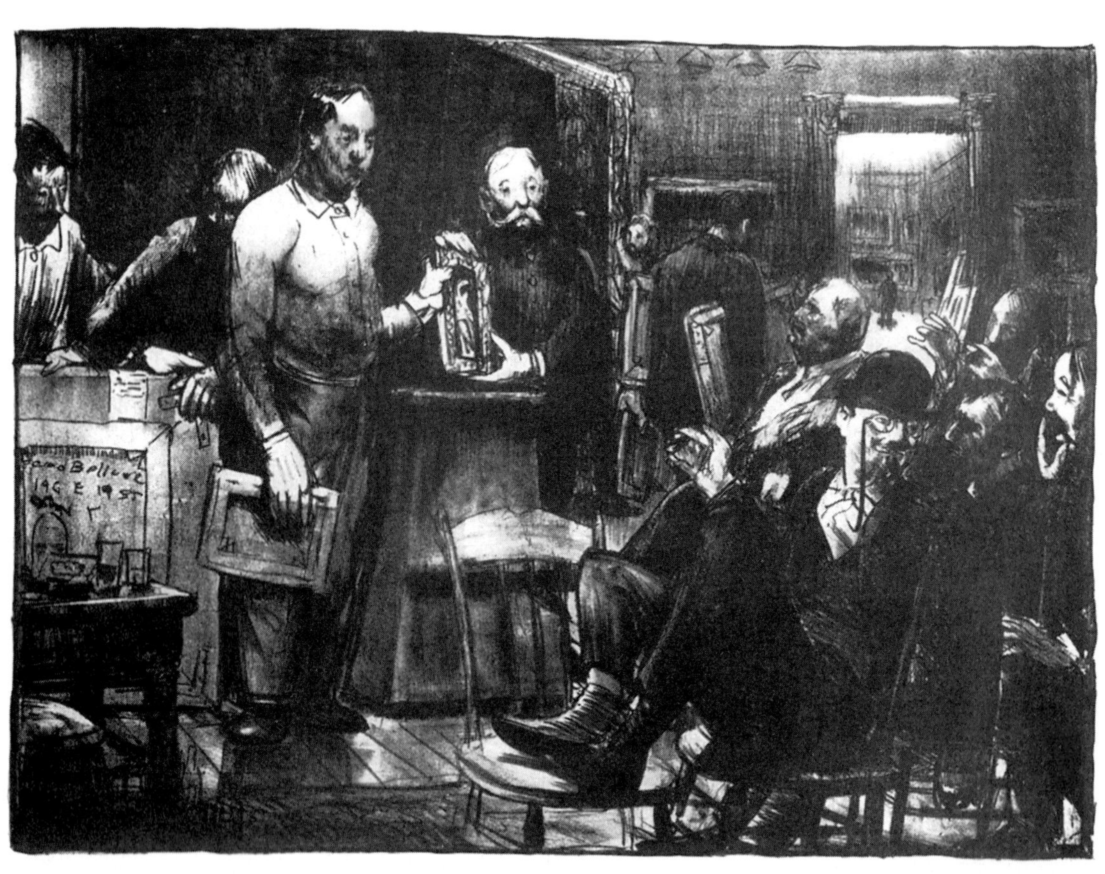

4   *The Jury*

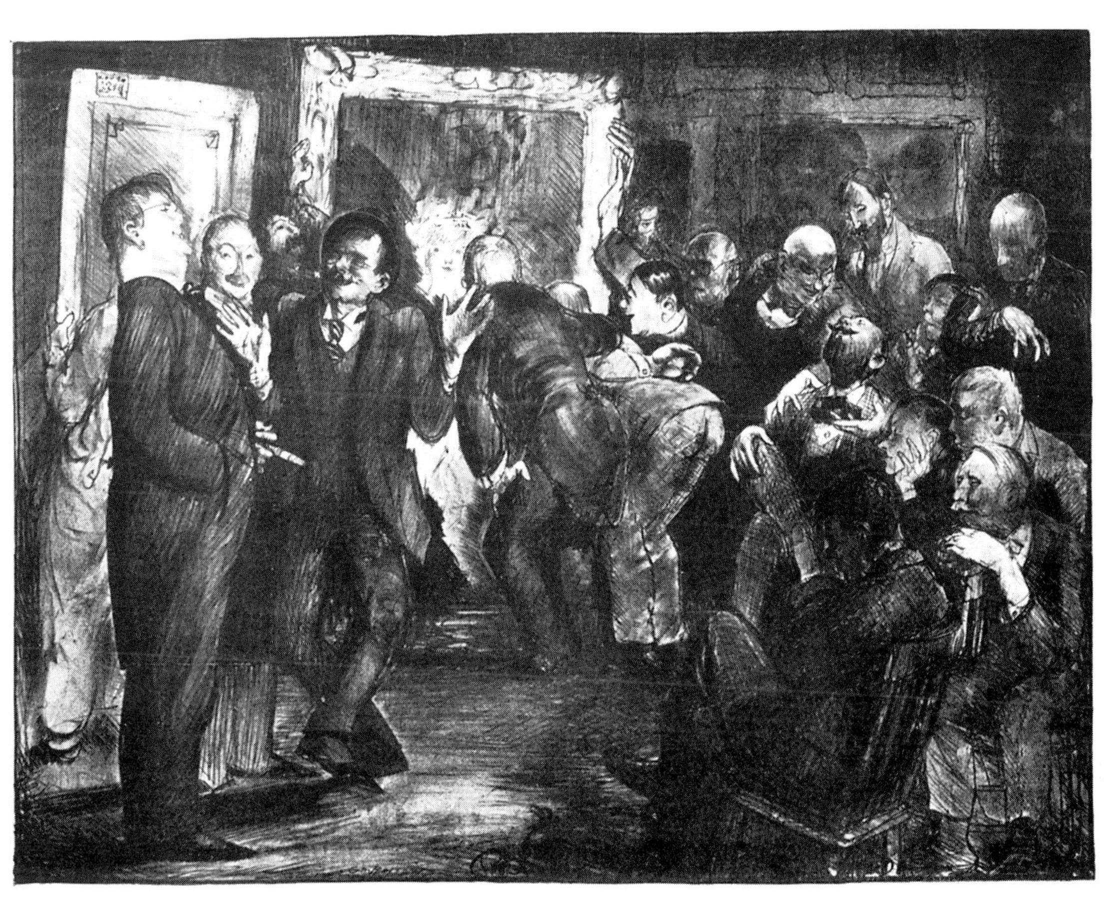

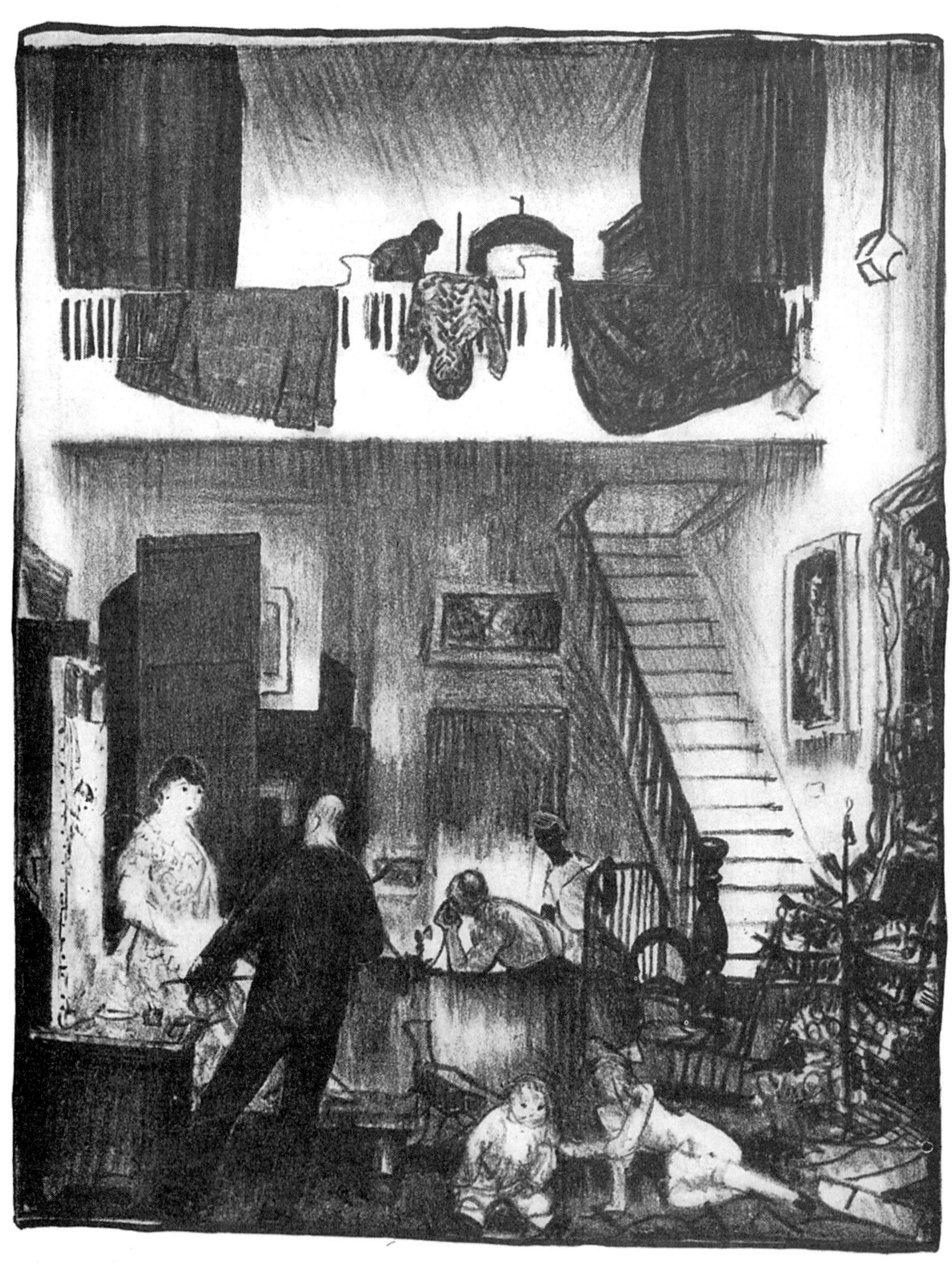

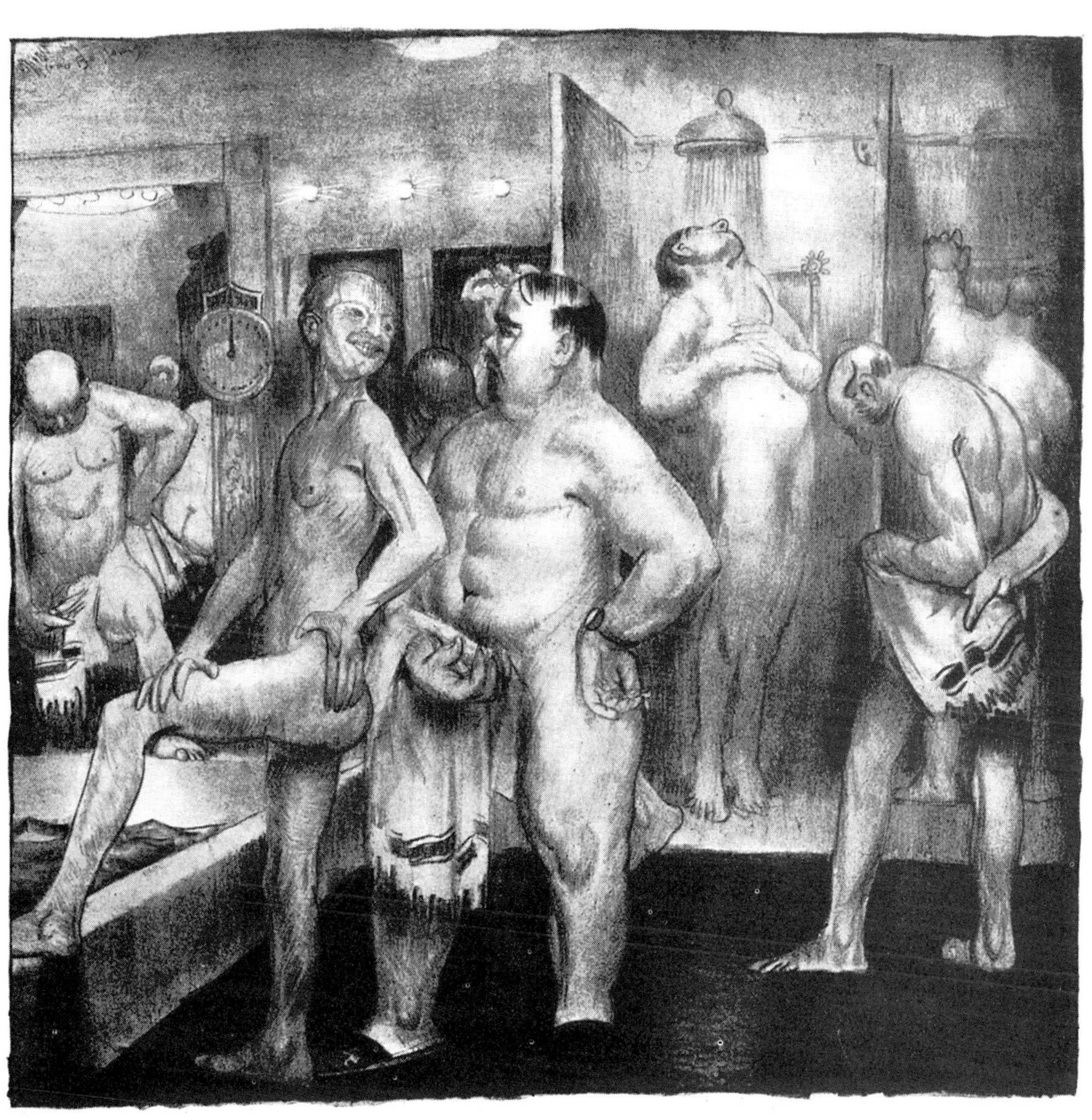

Shower-bath, Detail   7

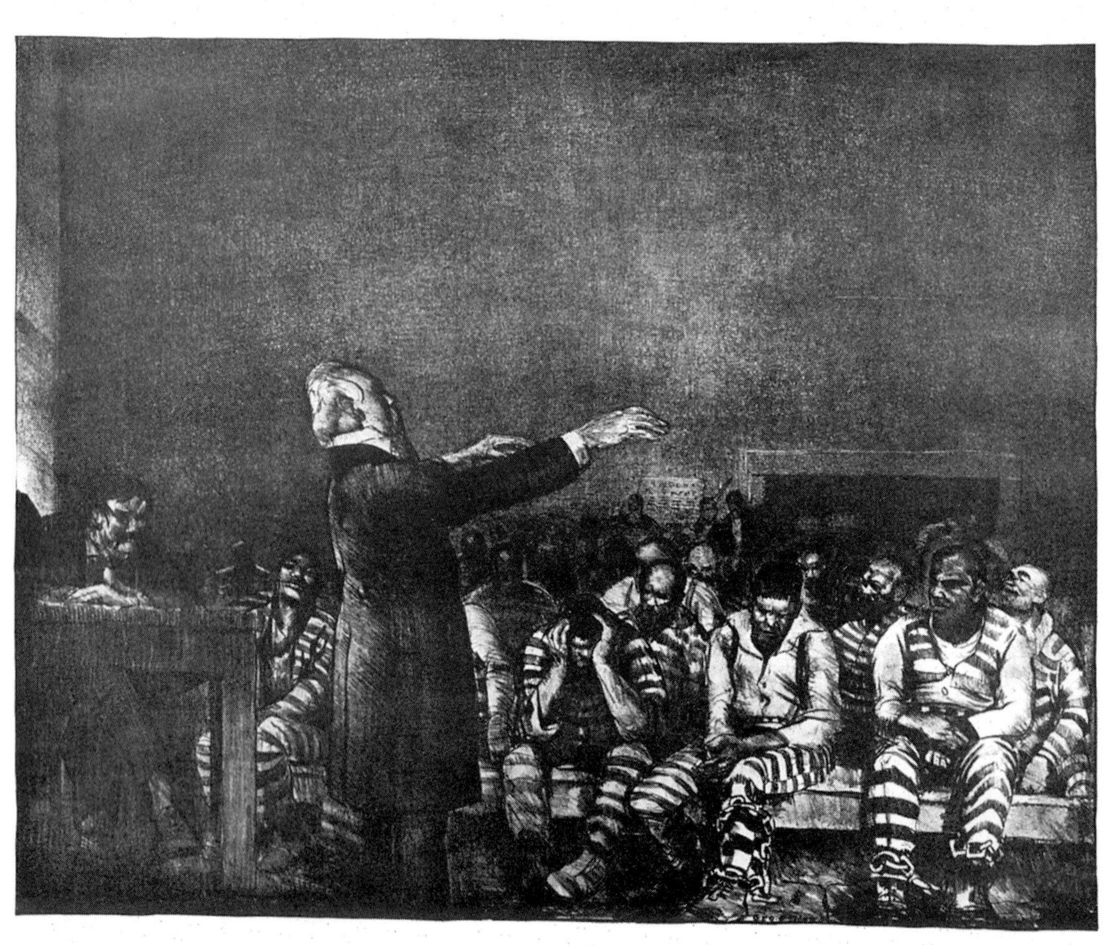

8   *Benediction in Georgia*

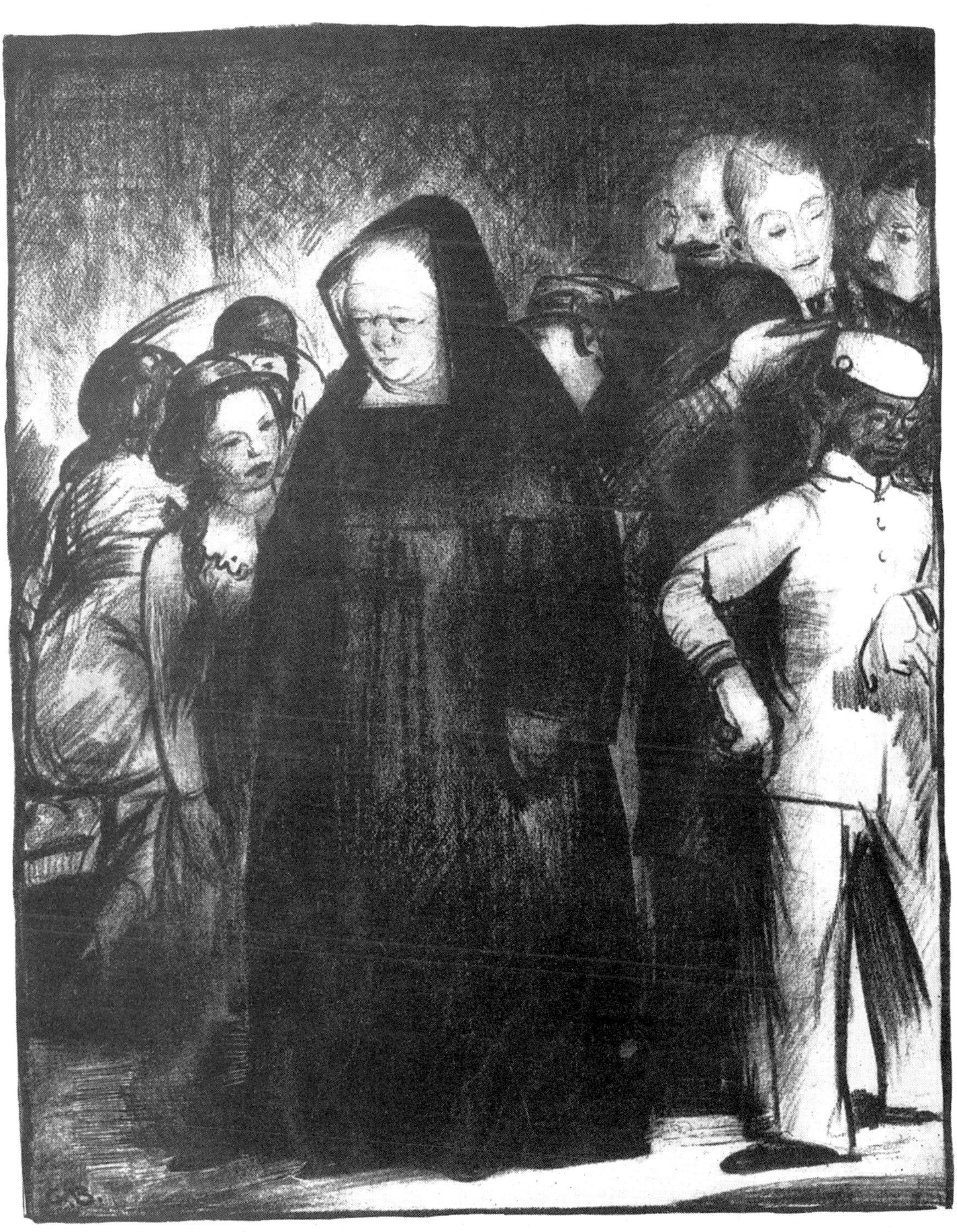

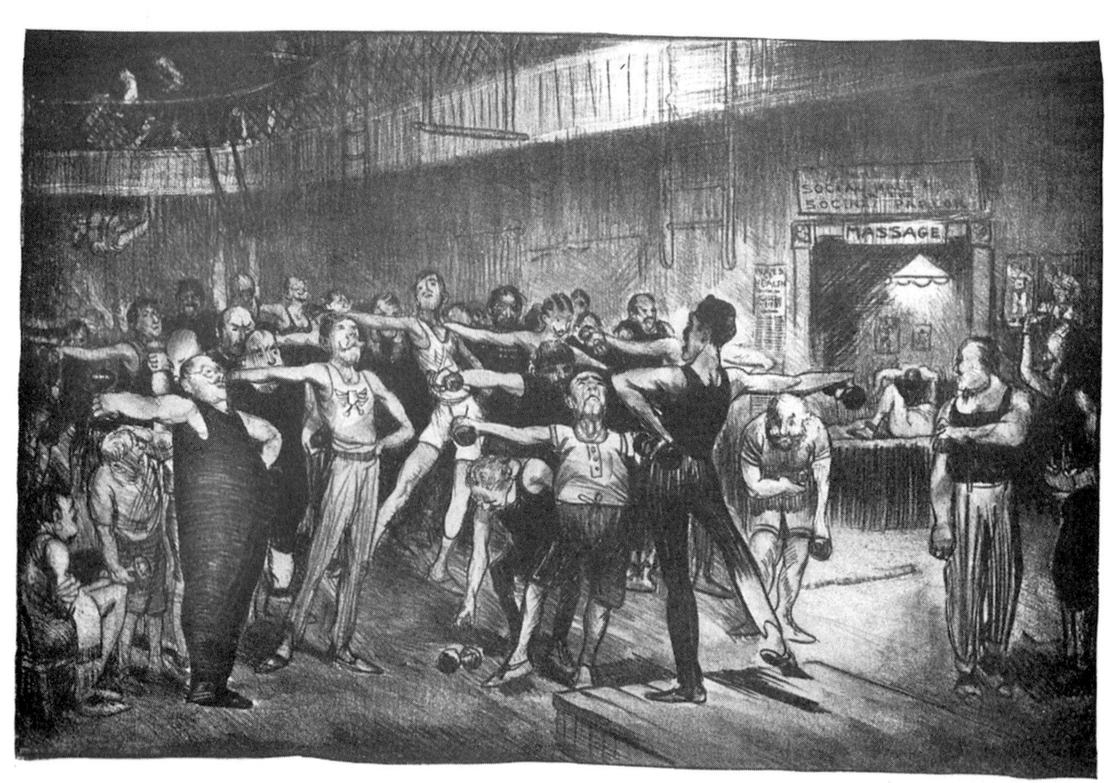

10   *Business-men's Class, Y.M.C.A.*

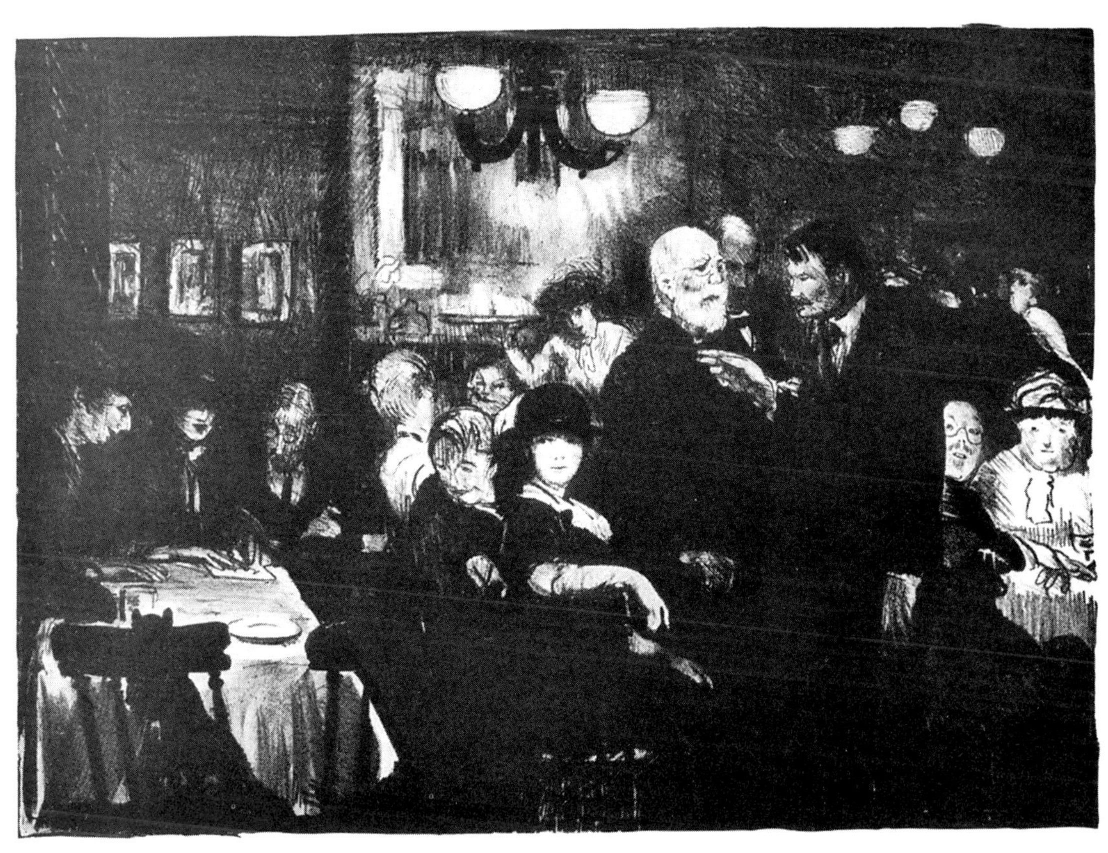

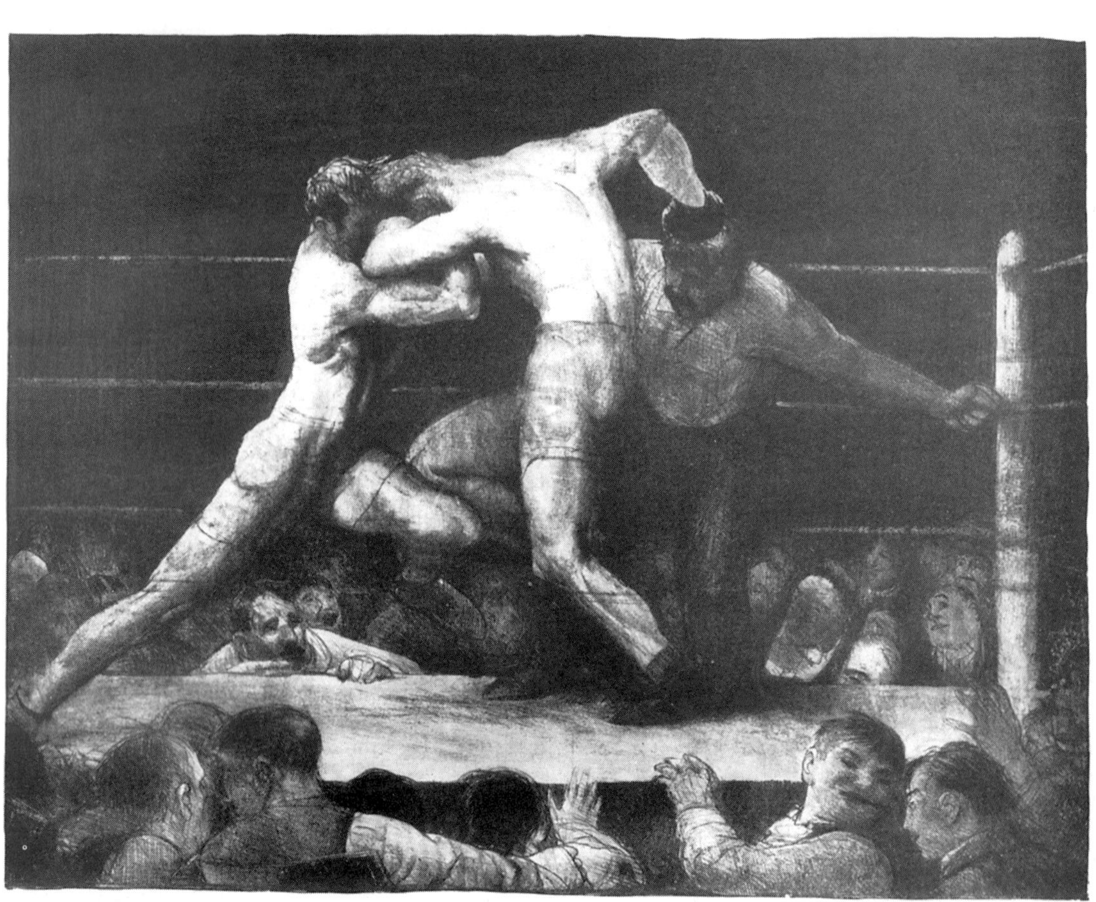

12   *Stag at Sharkey's*

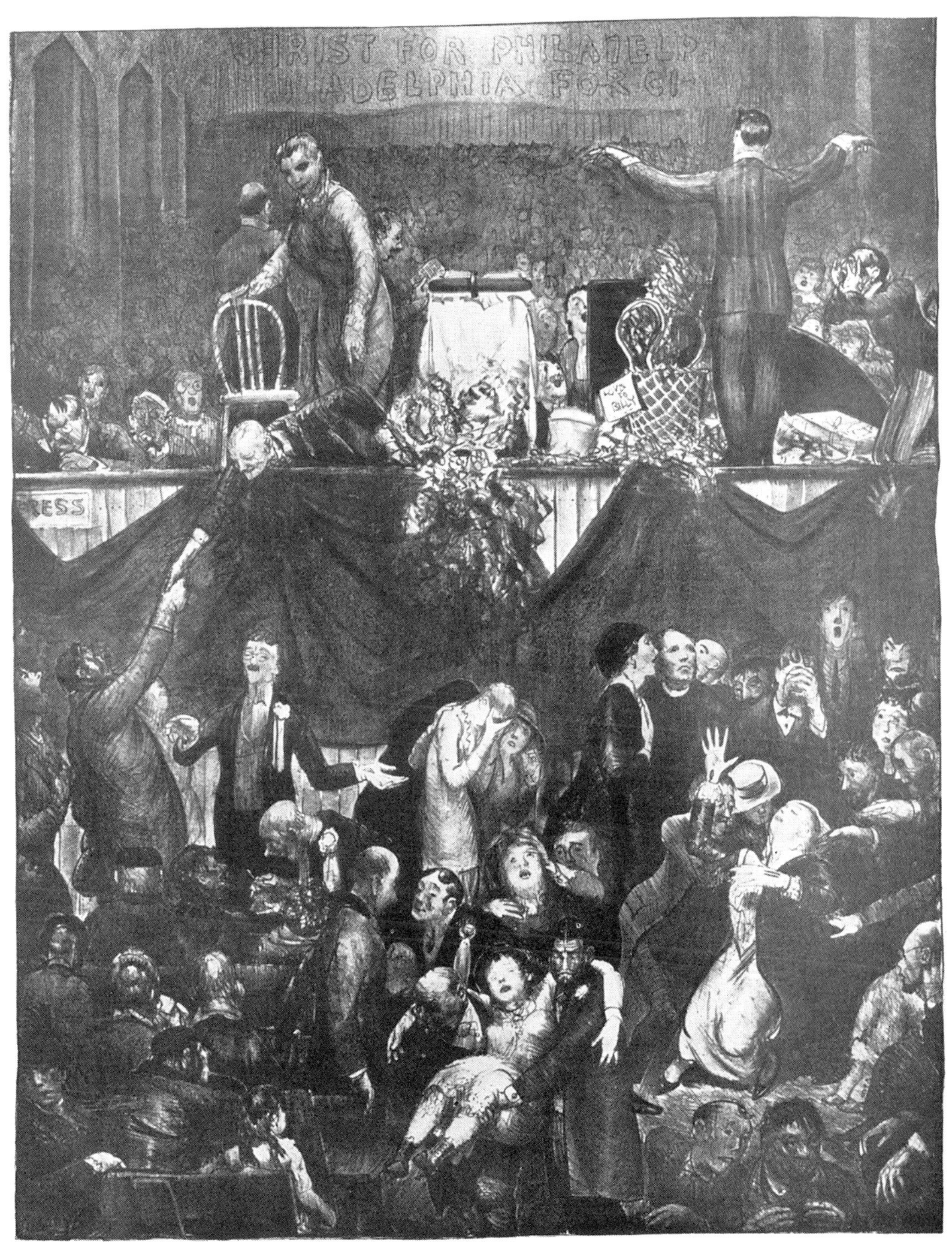
CHRIST FOR PHILADELPHIA
PHILADELPHIA FOR CHRIST

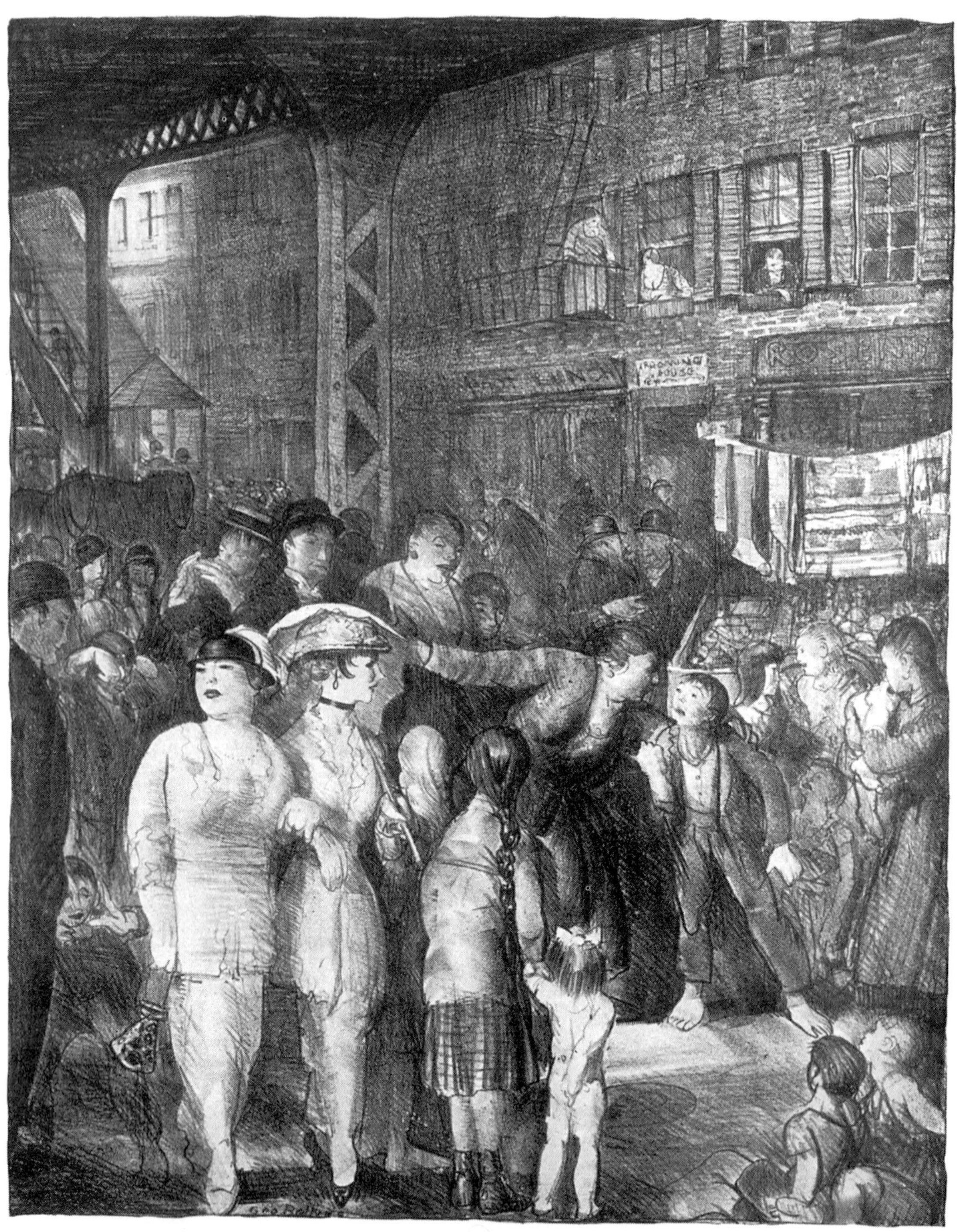

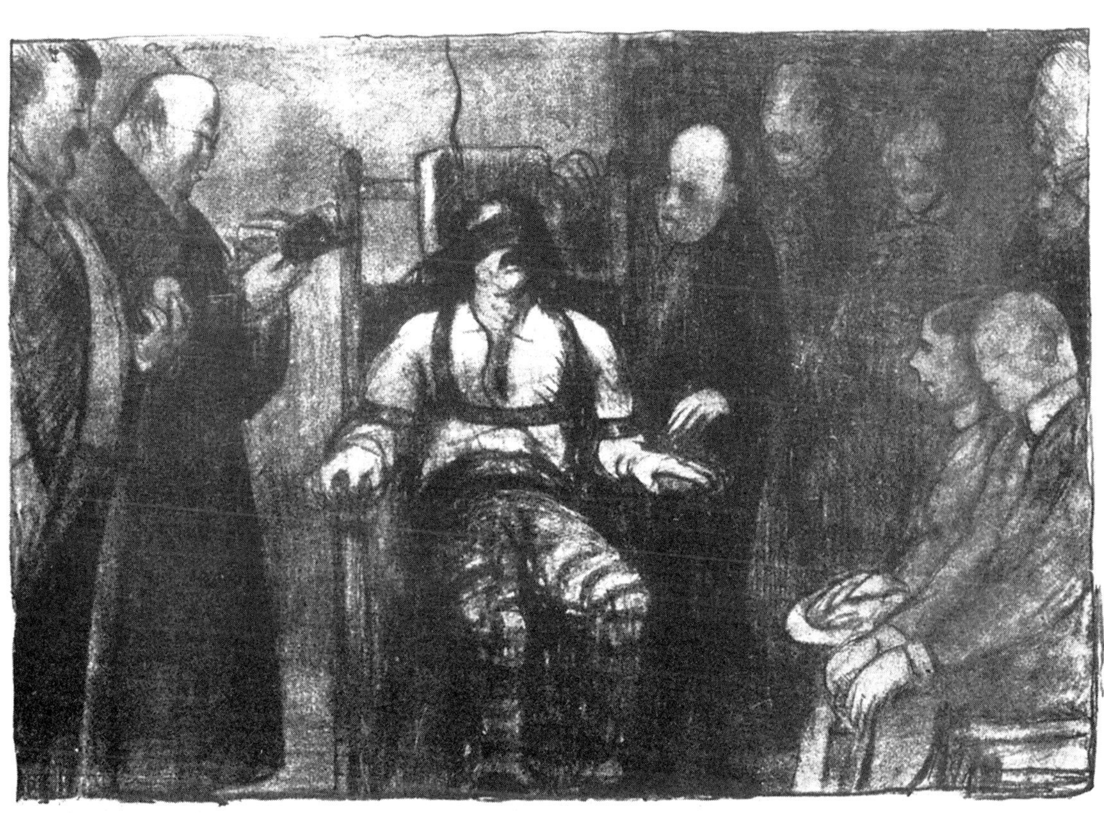

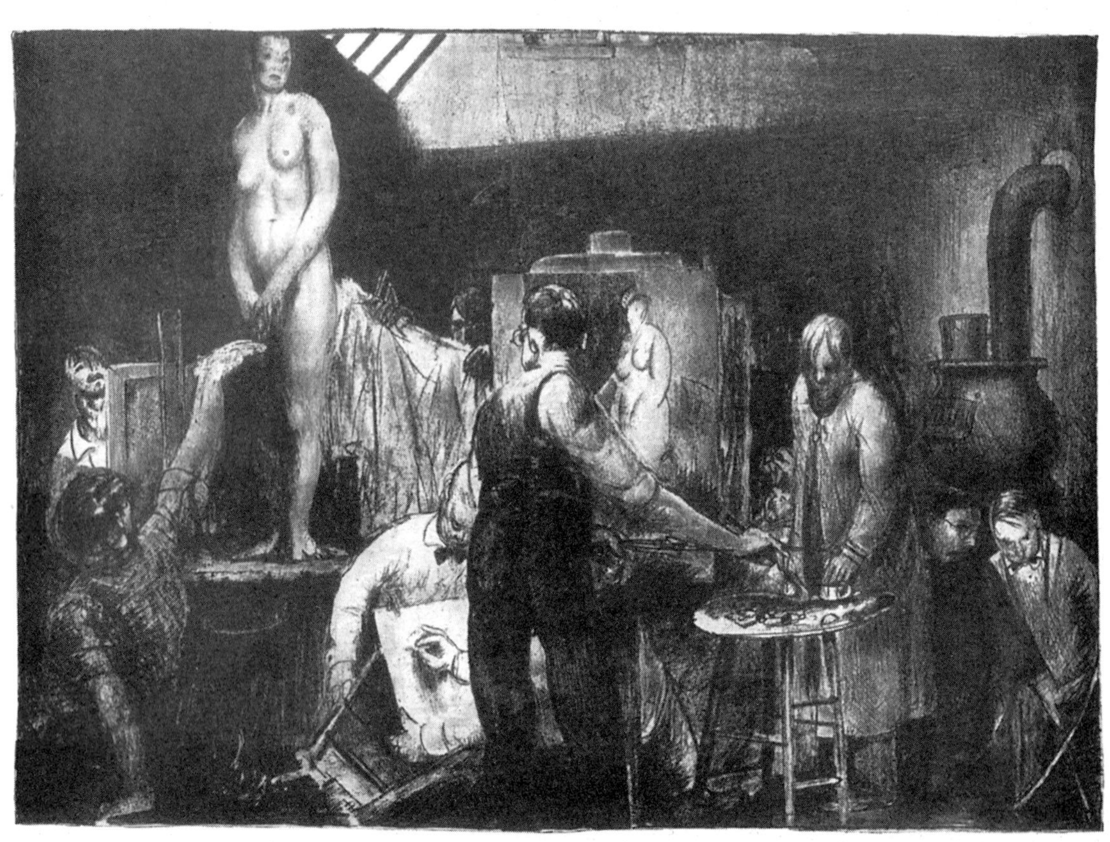

16   *The Life Class*

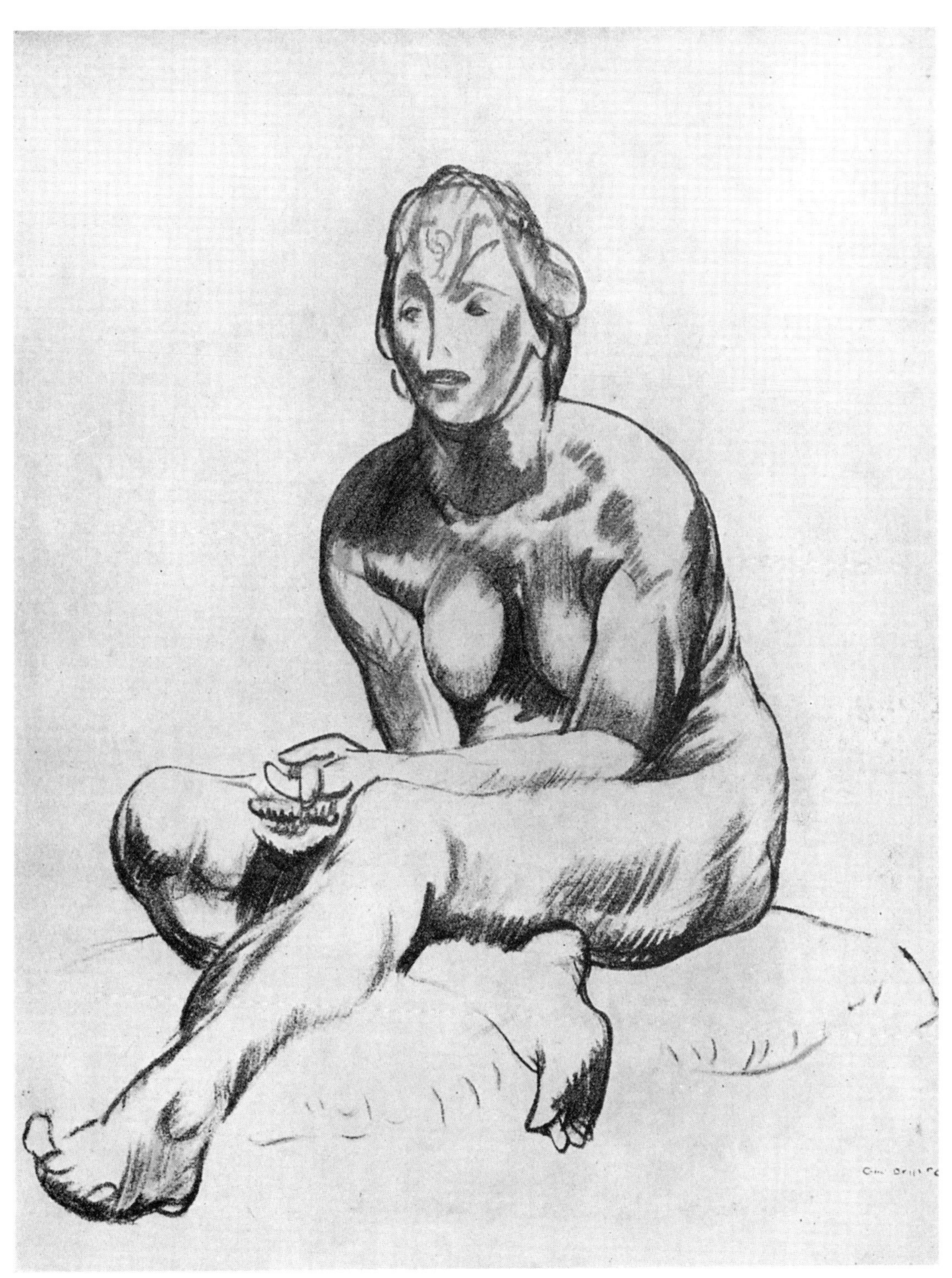

Life Study, Nude Woman Seated   17

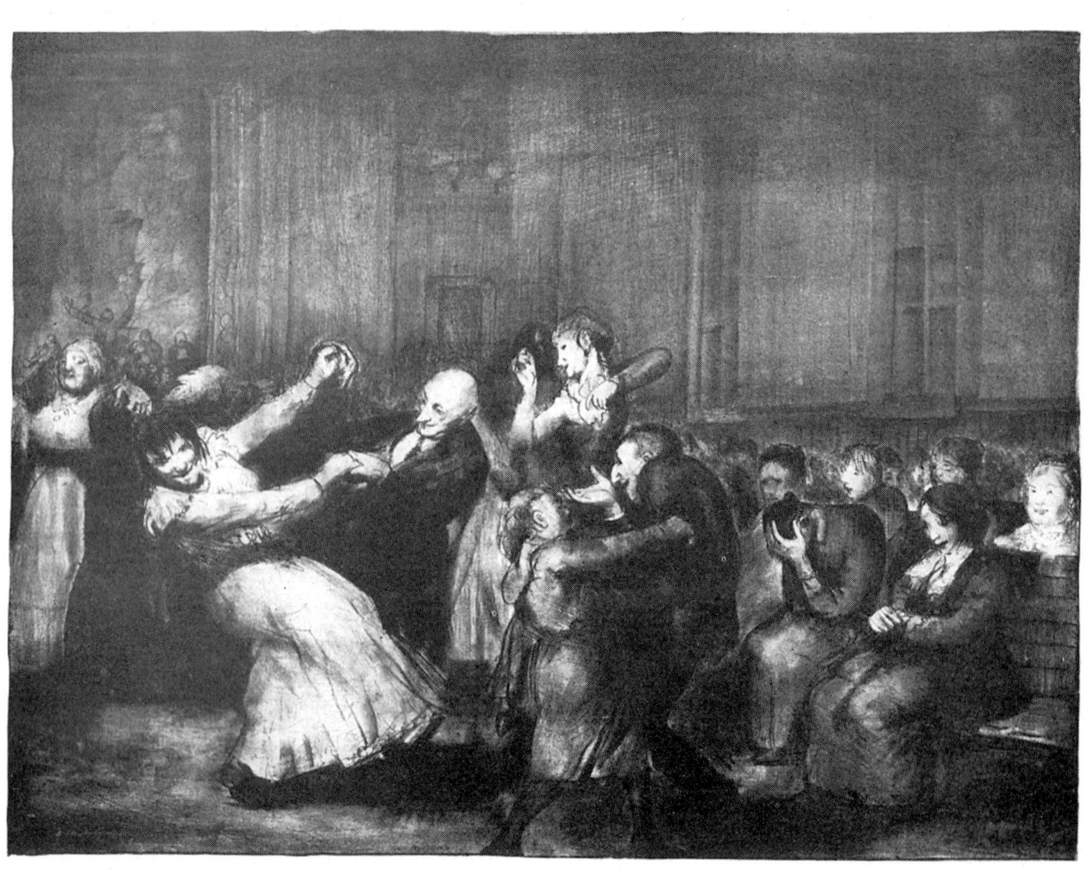

18   *Dance in a Madhouse*

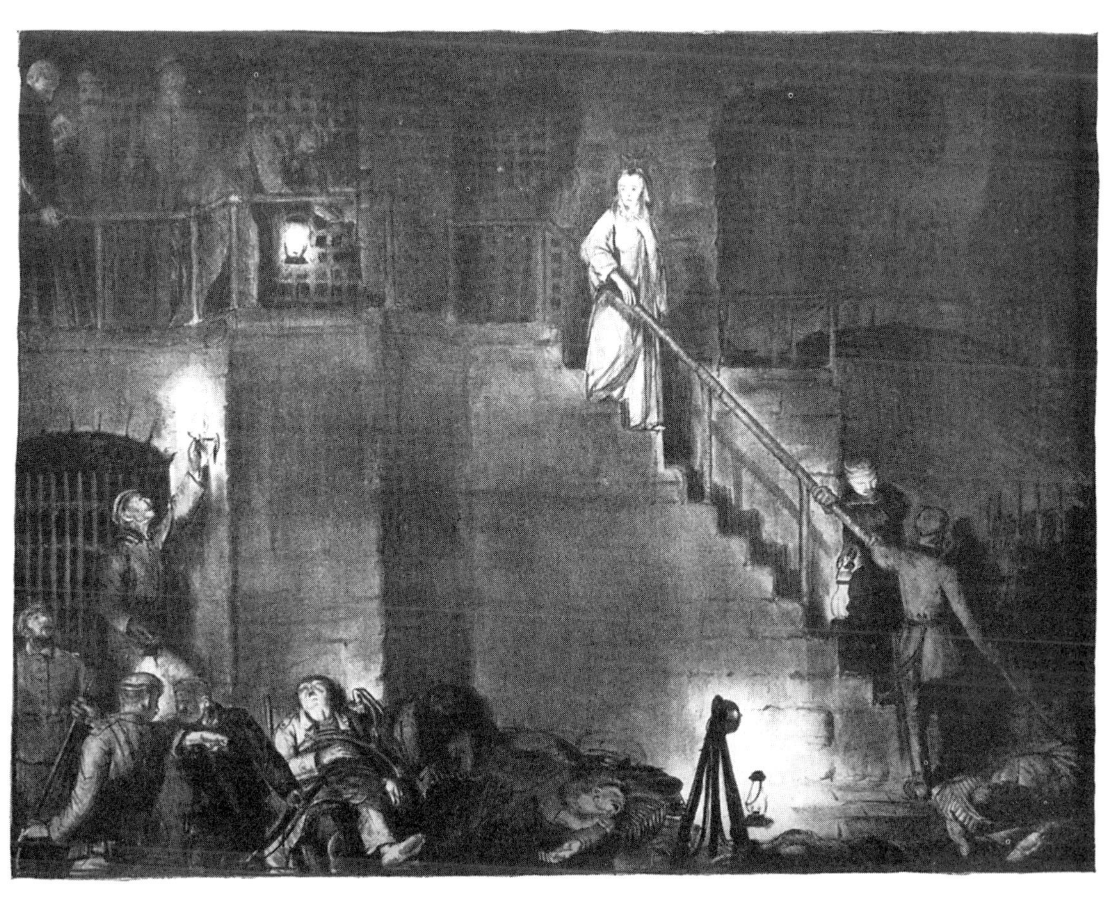

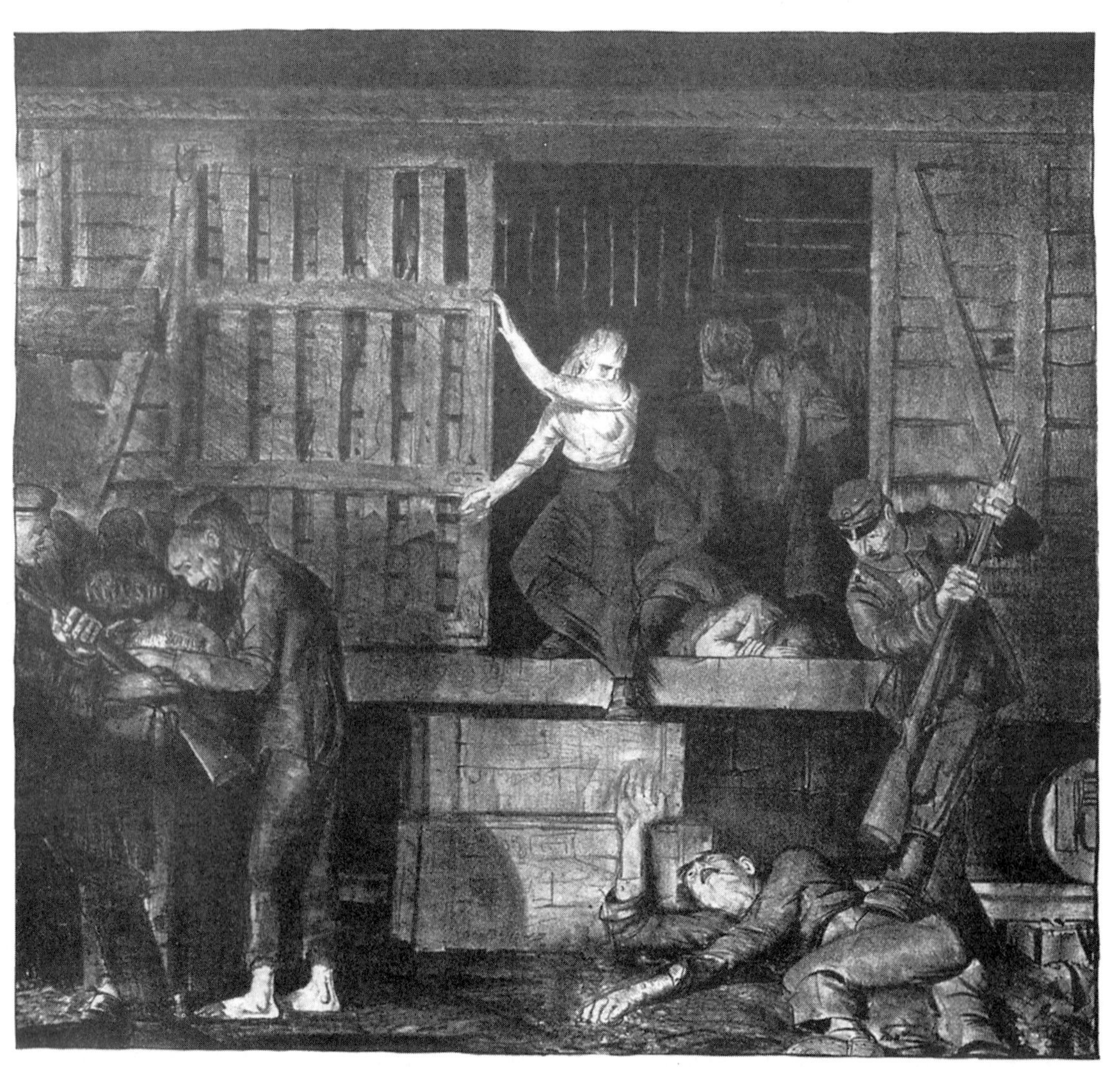

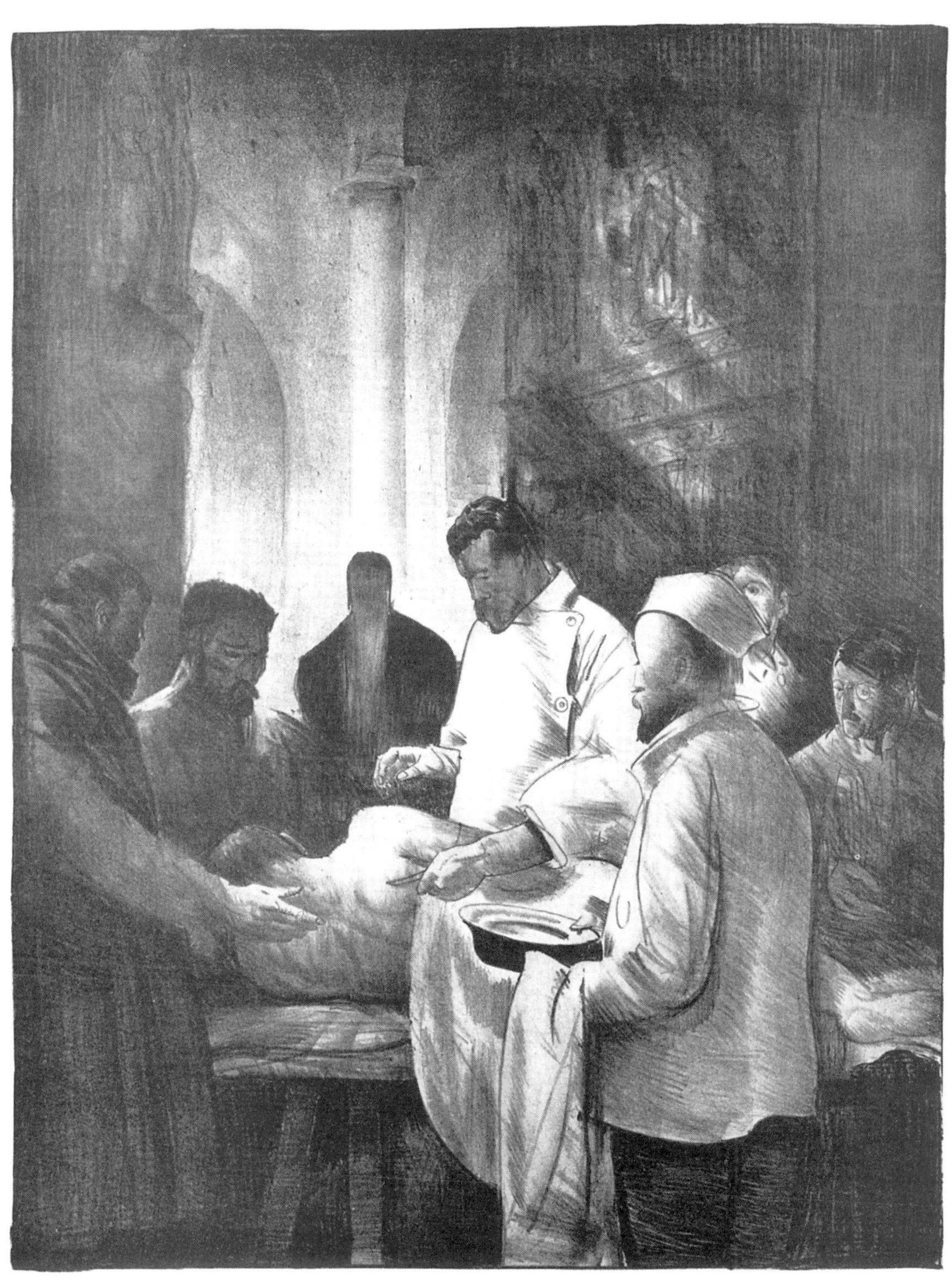

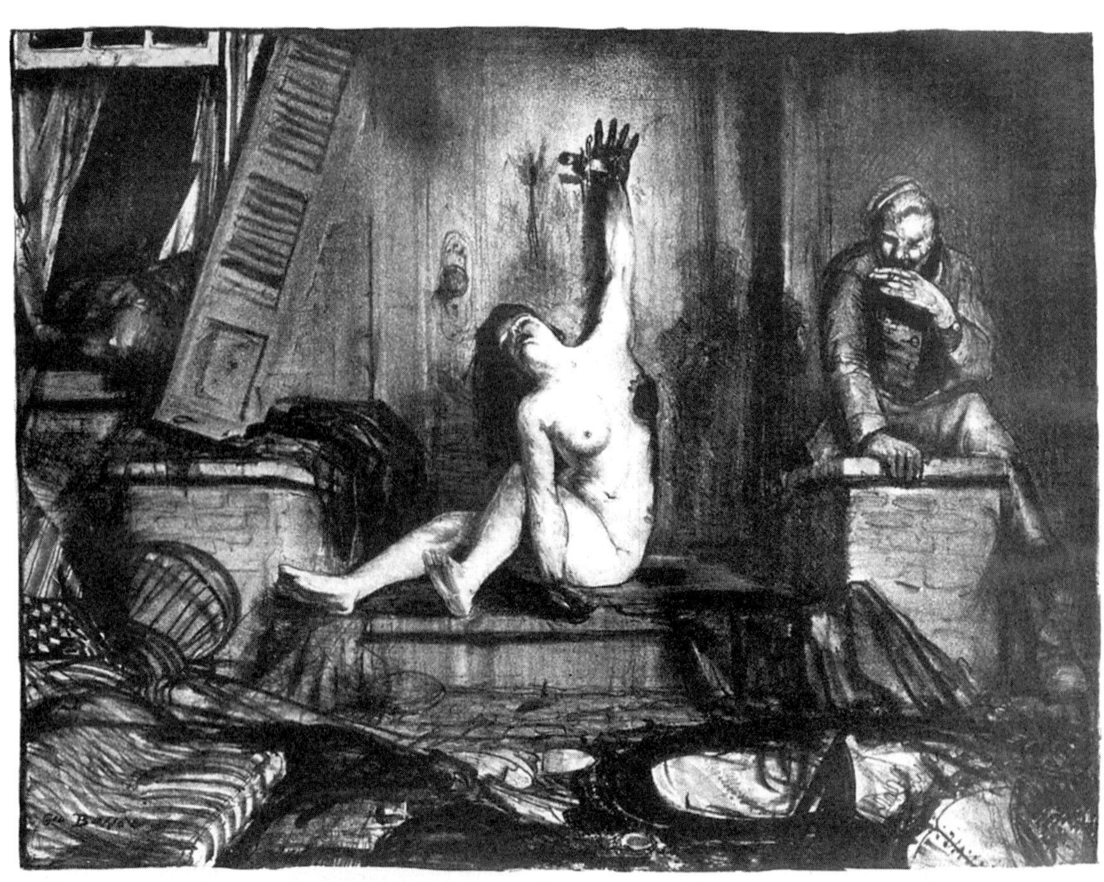

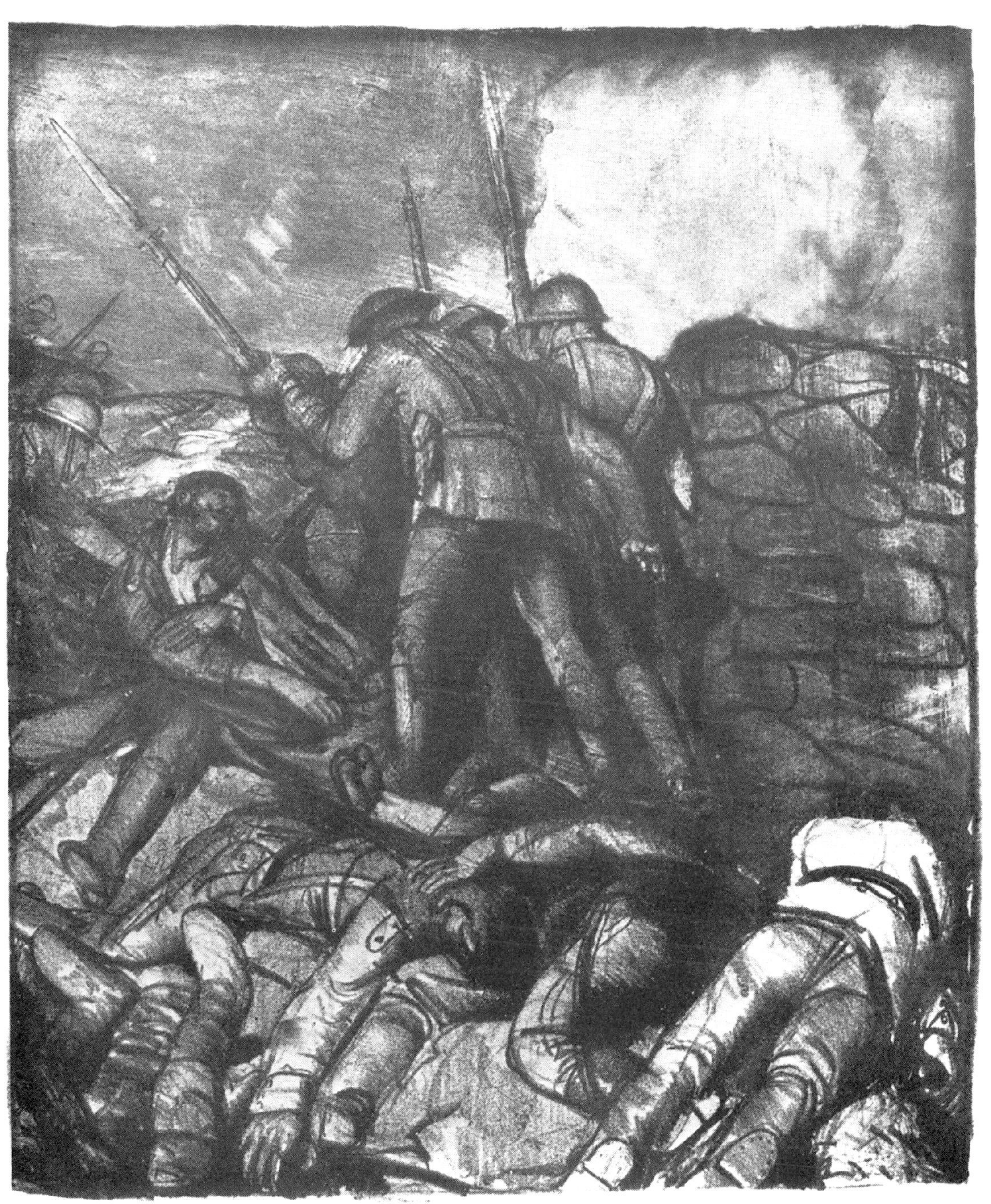

The Charge, Detail   23

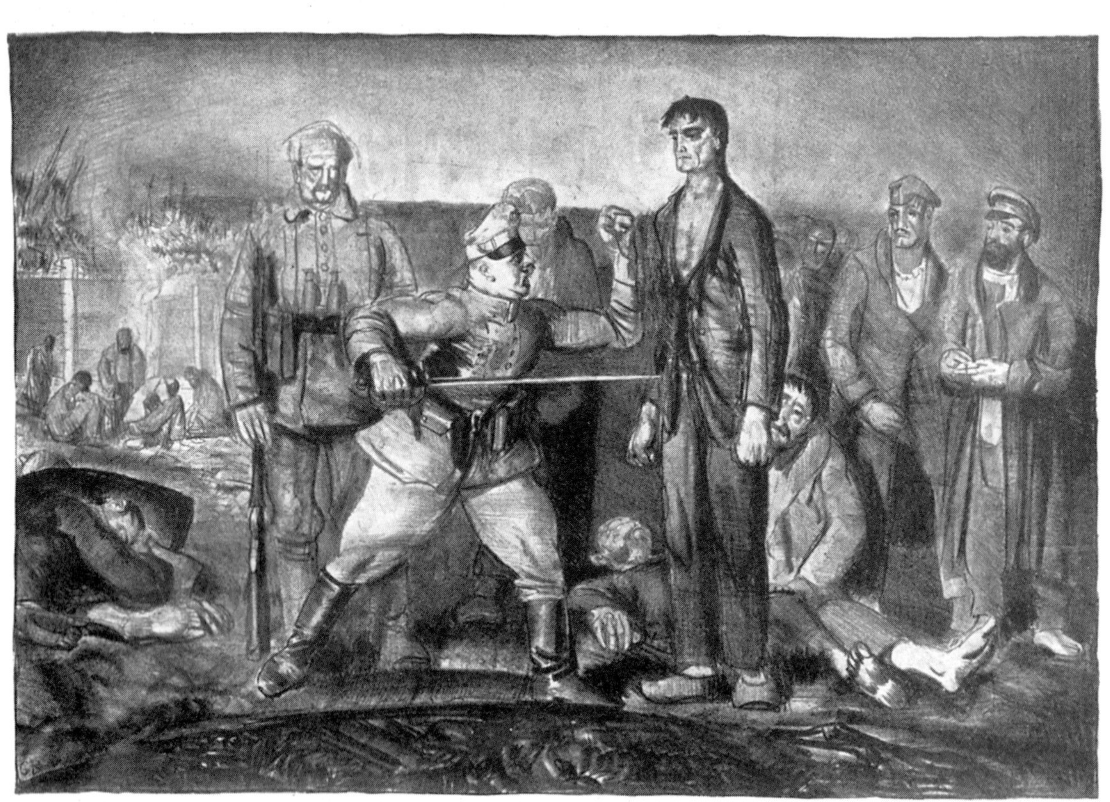

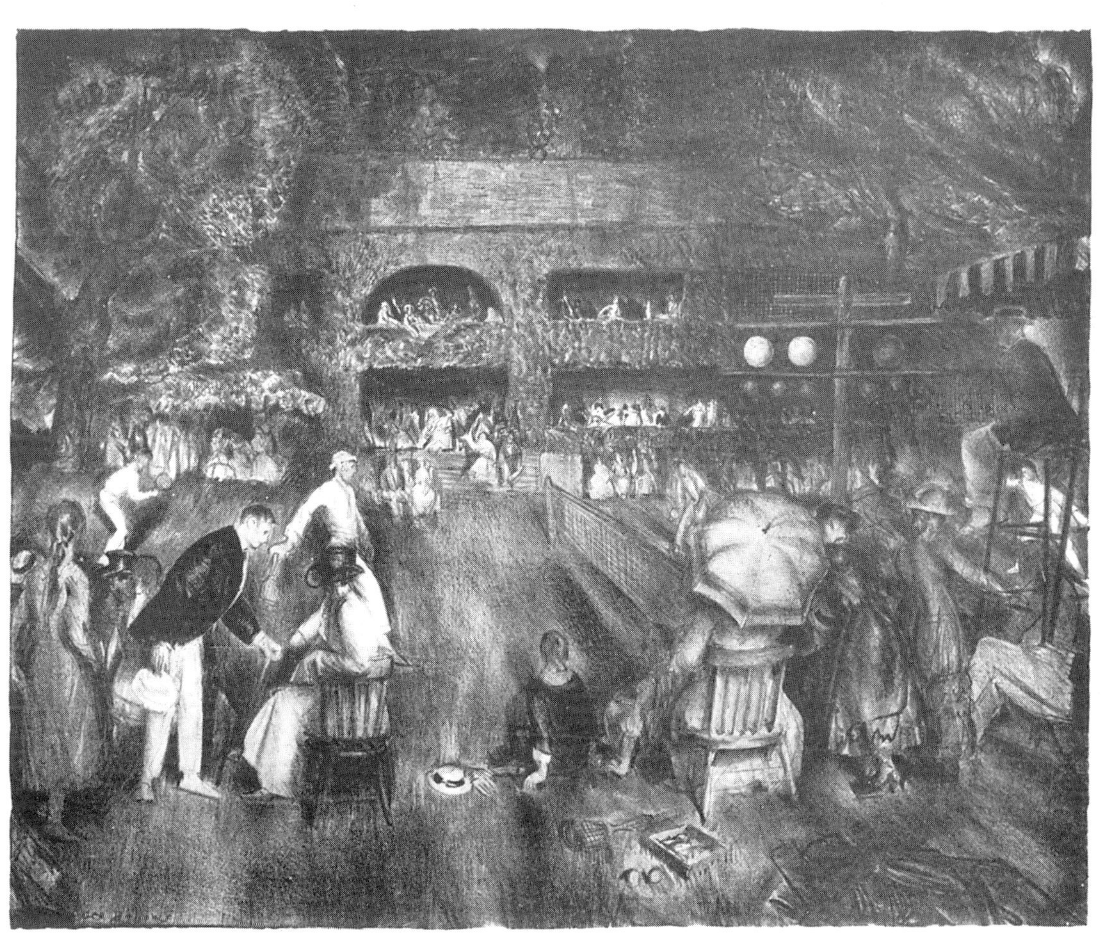

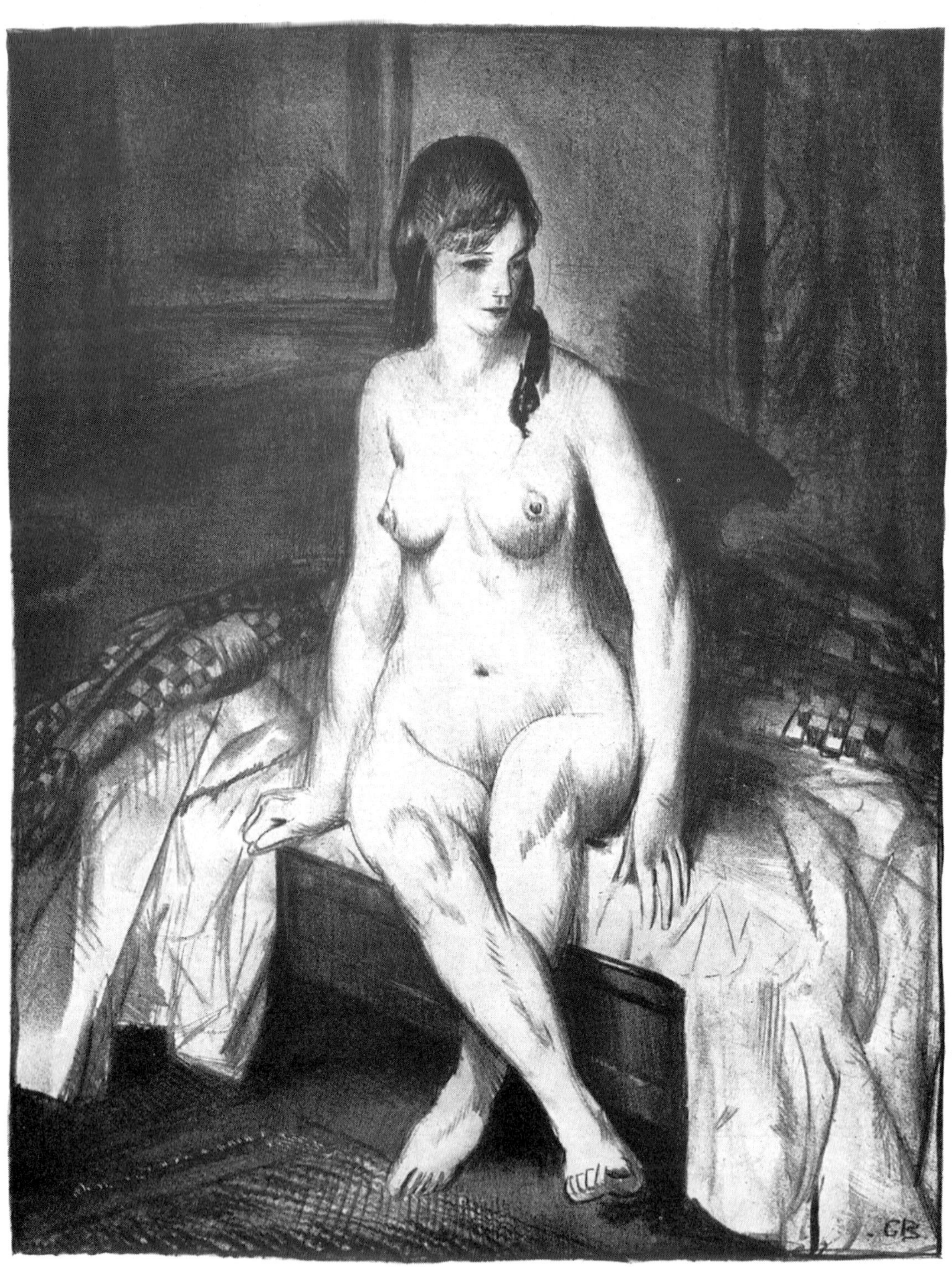

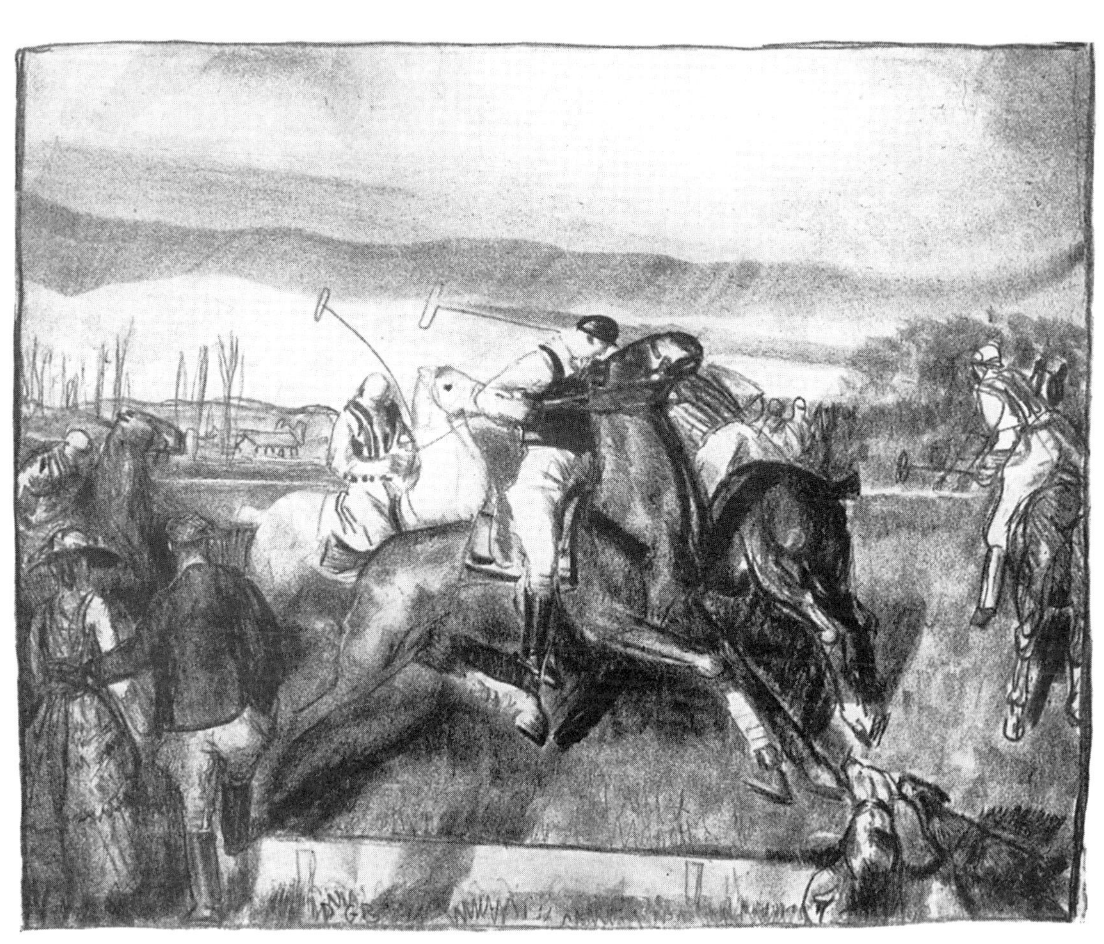

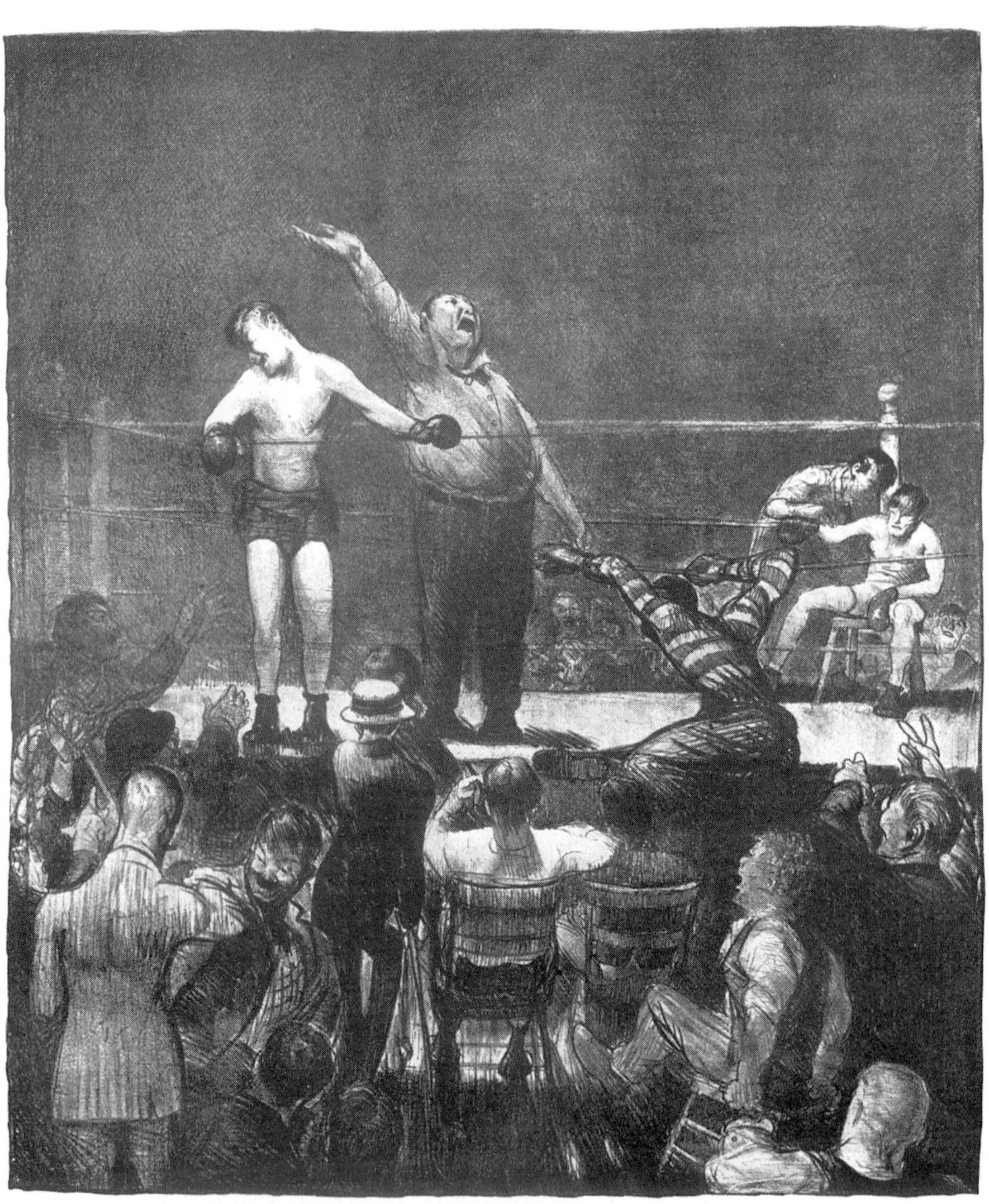

28   *Introducing the Champion, Small, No. 2*

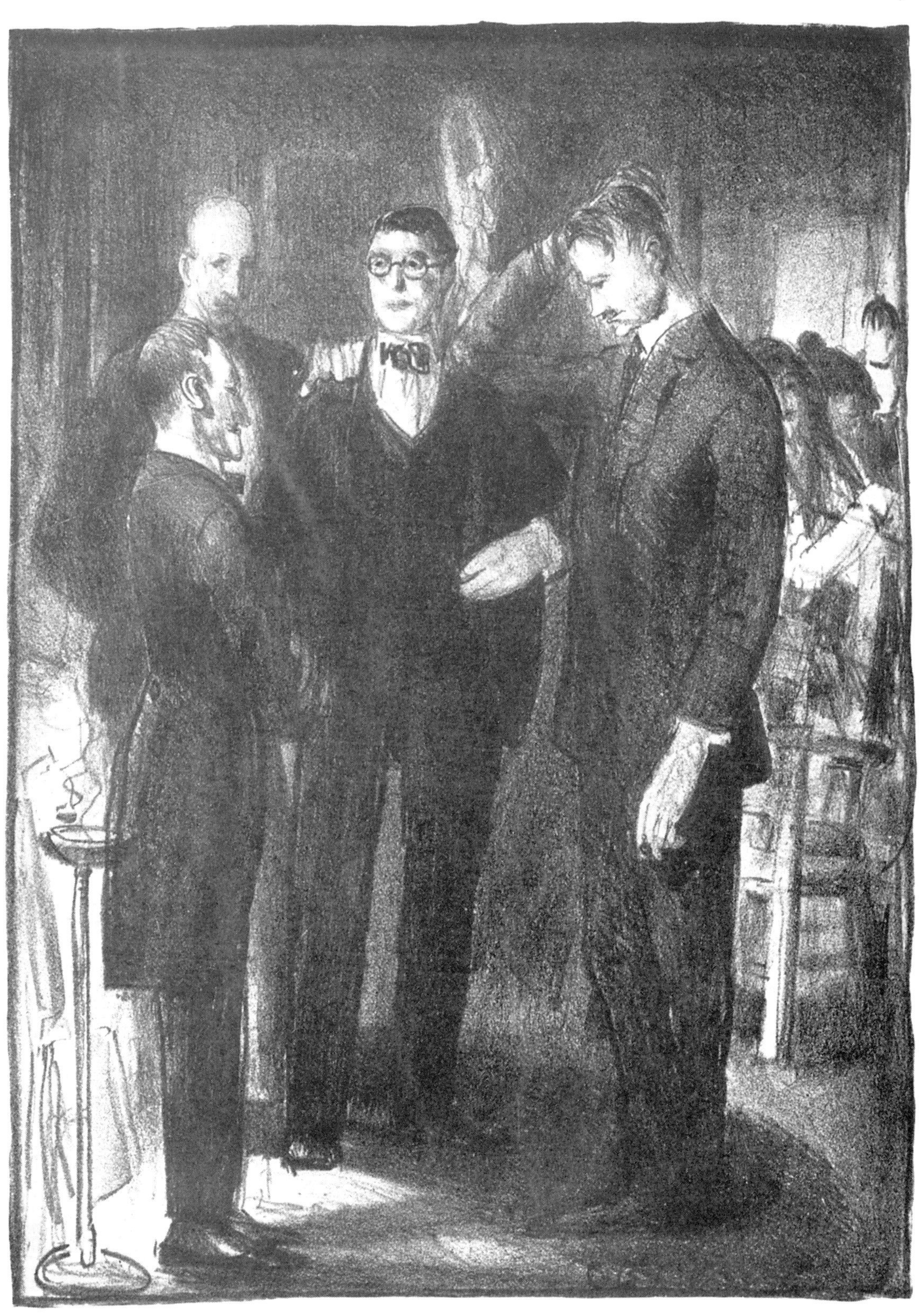

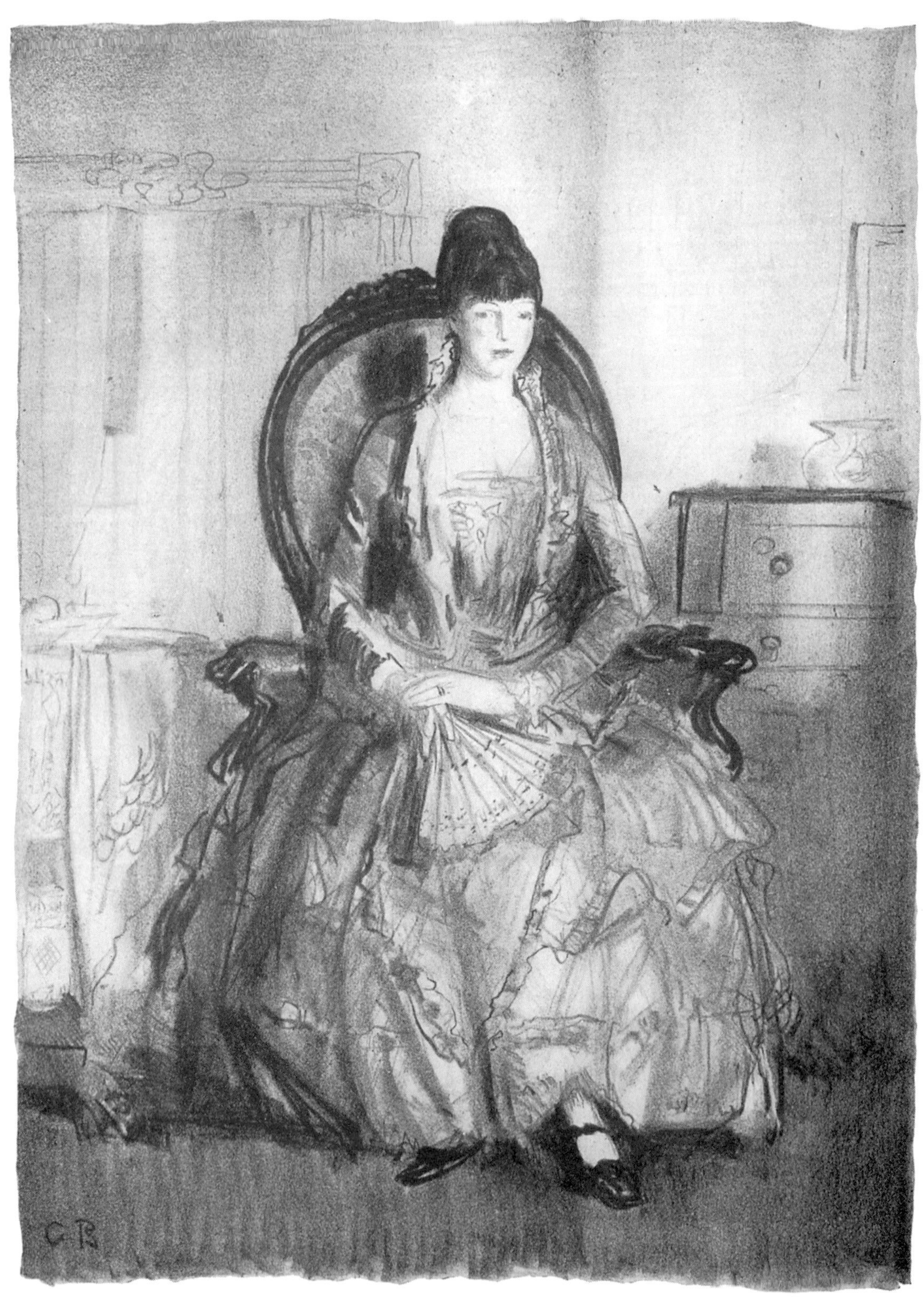

  Emma in a Chair, or Lady with a Fan

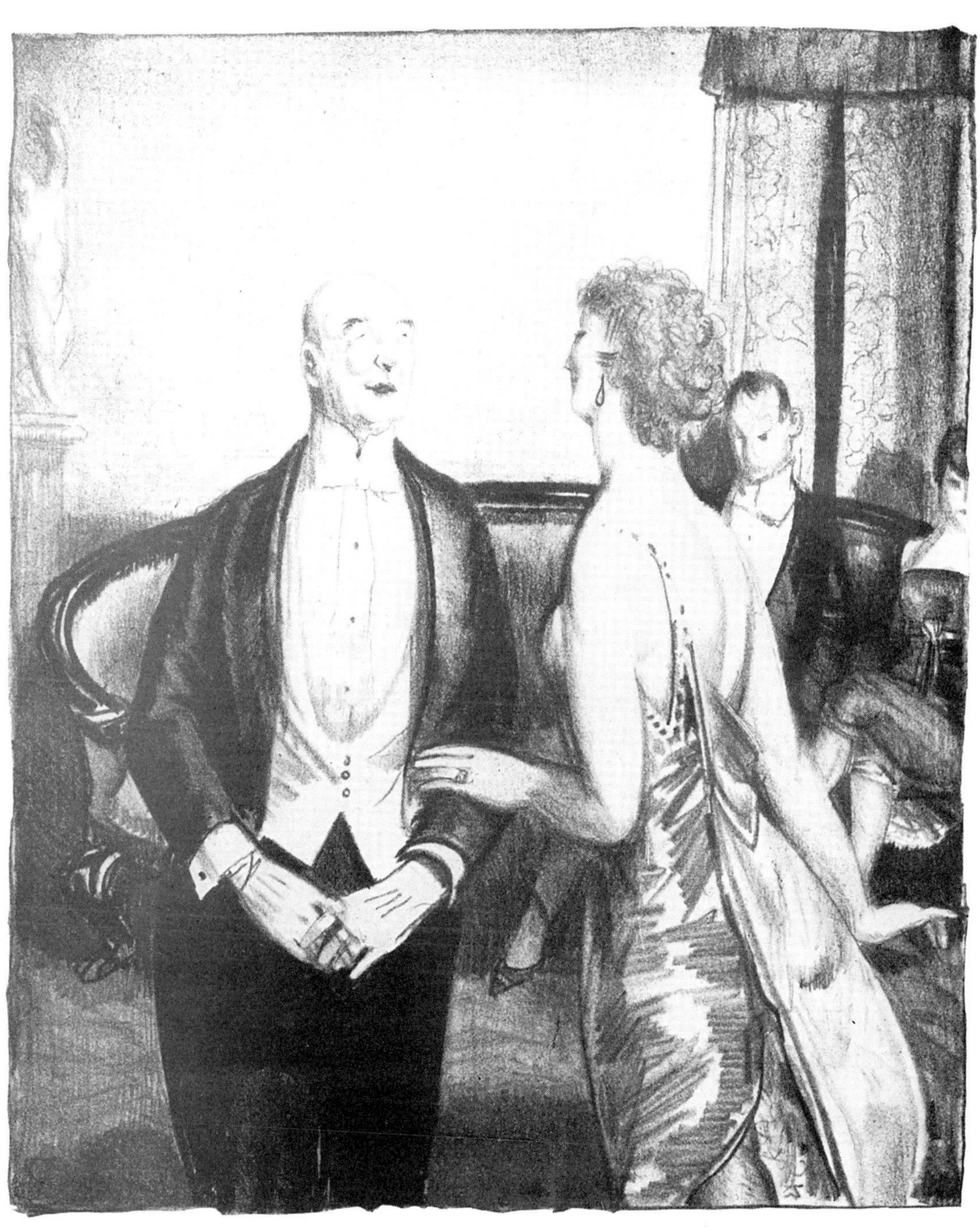

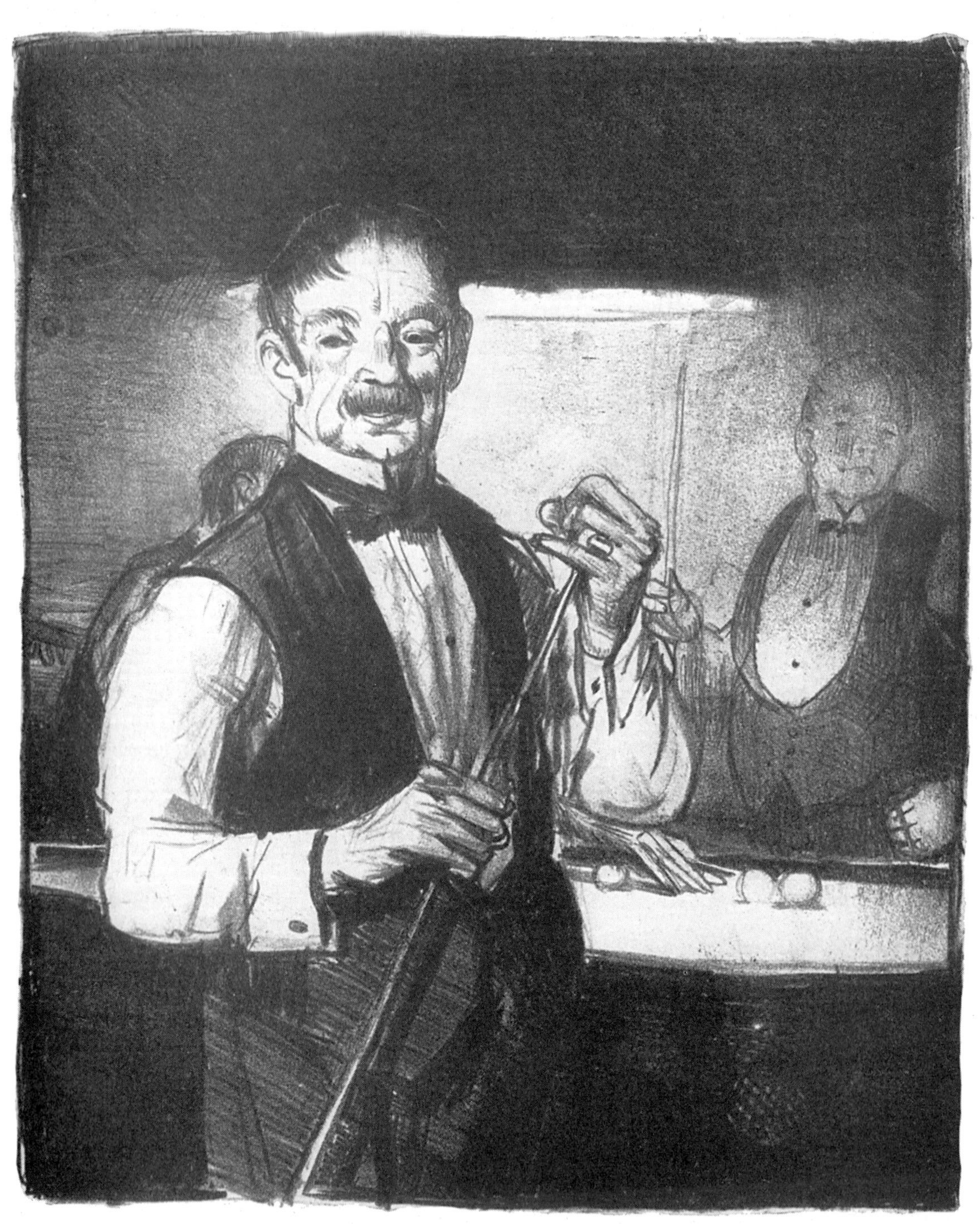

32   *Old Billiard-player*

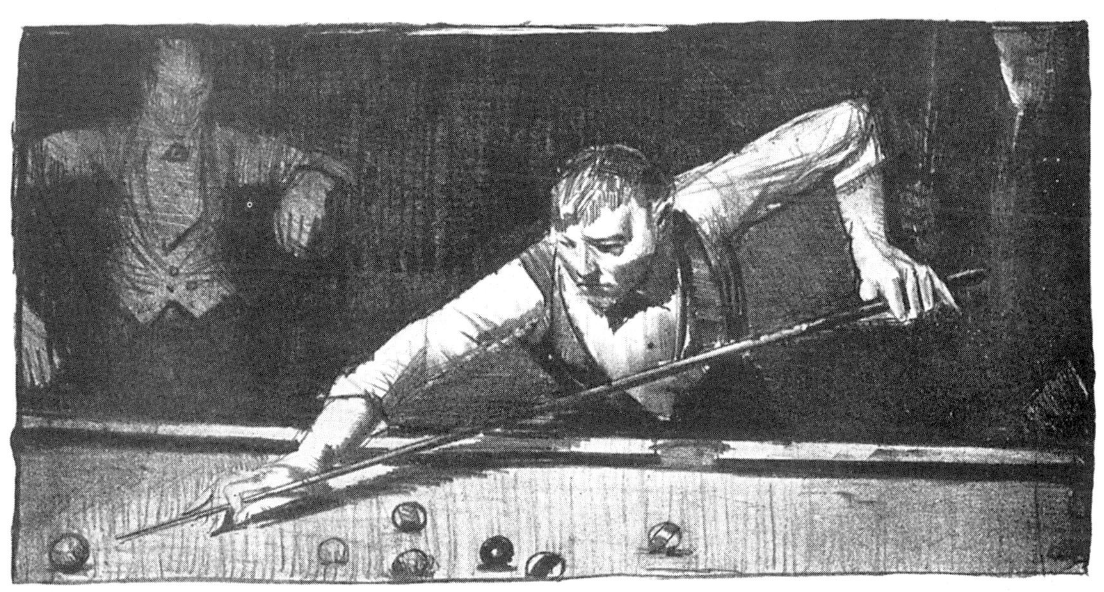

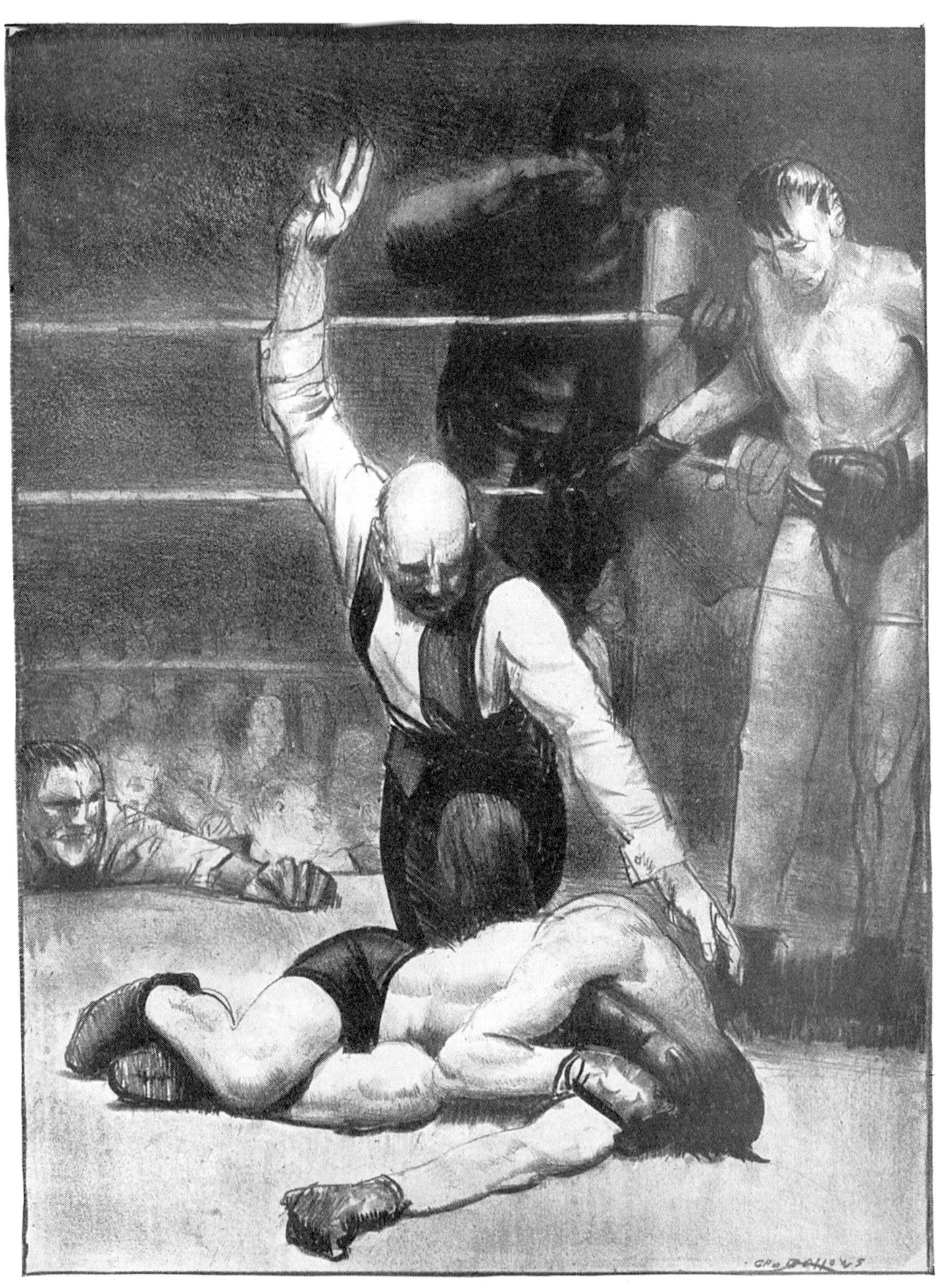

34   *Counted Out, No. 2*

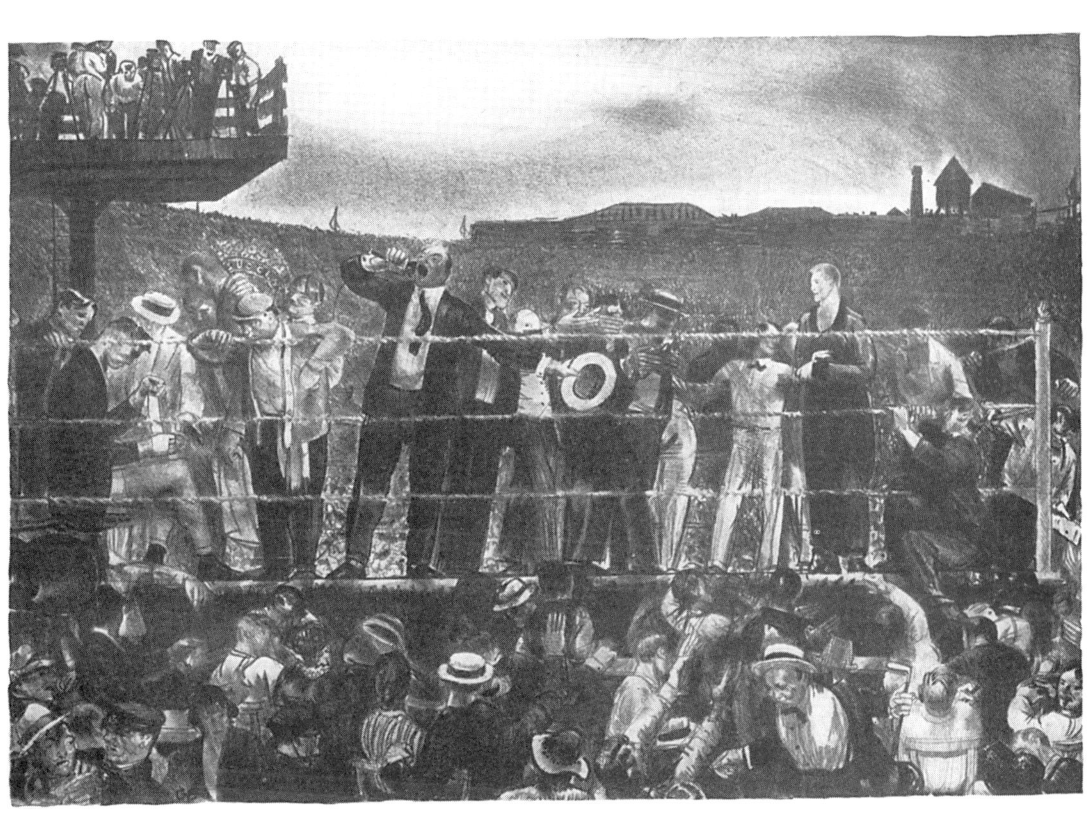

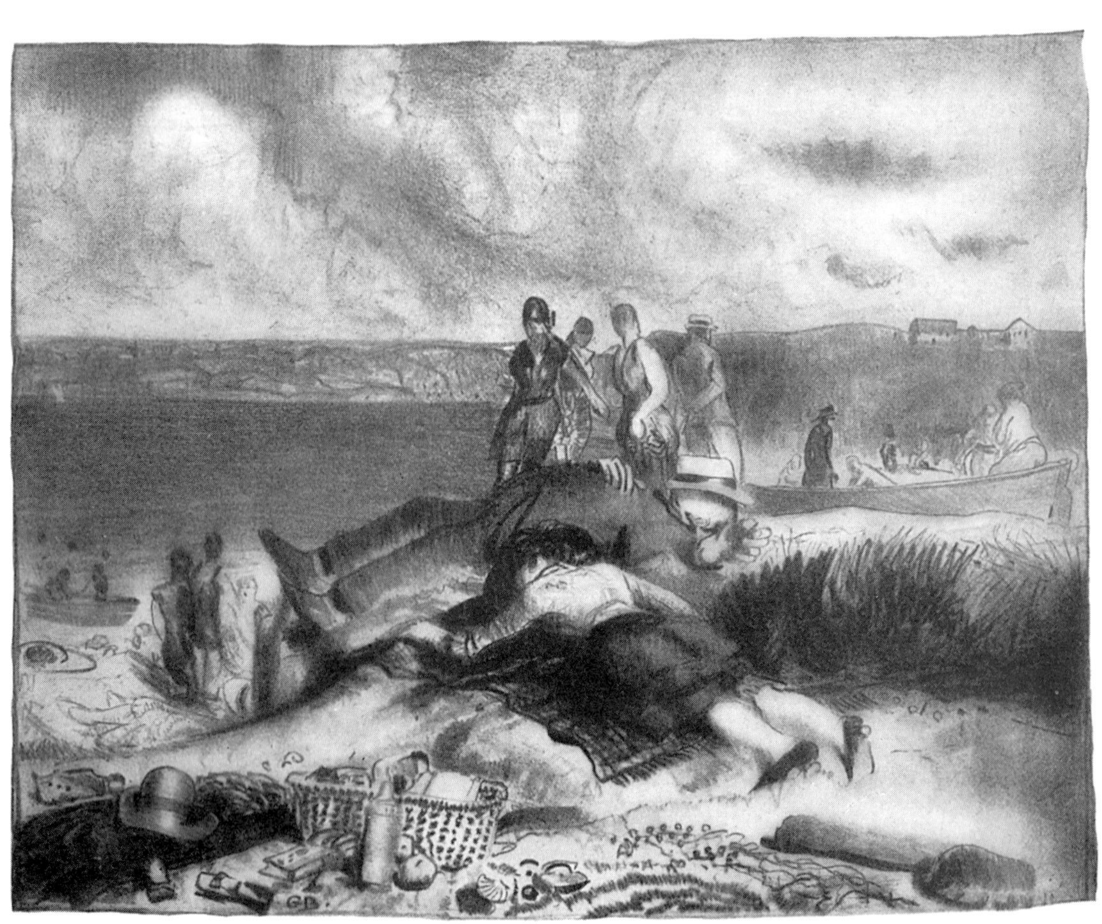

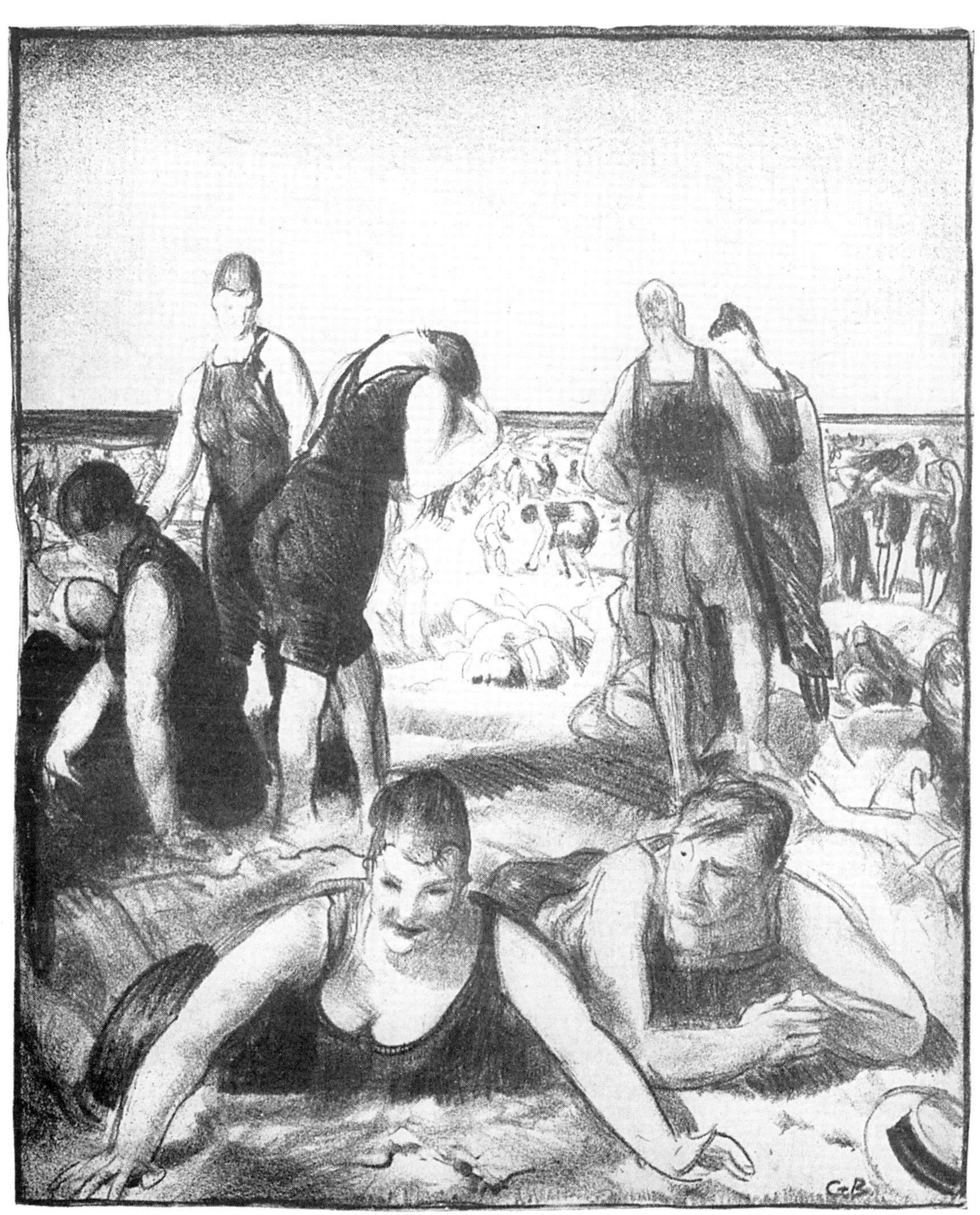

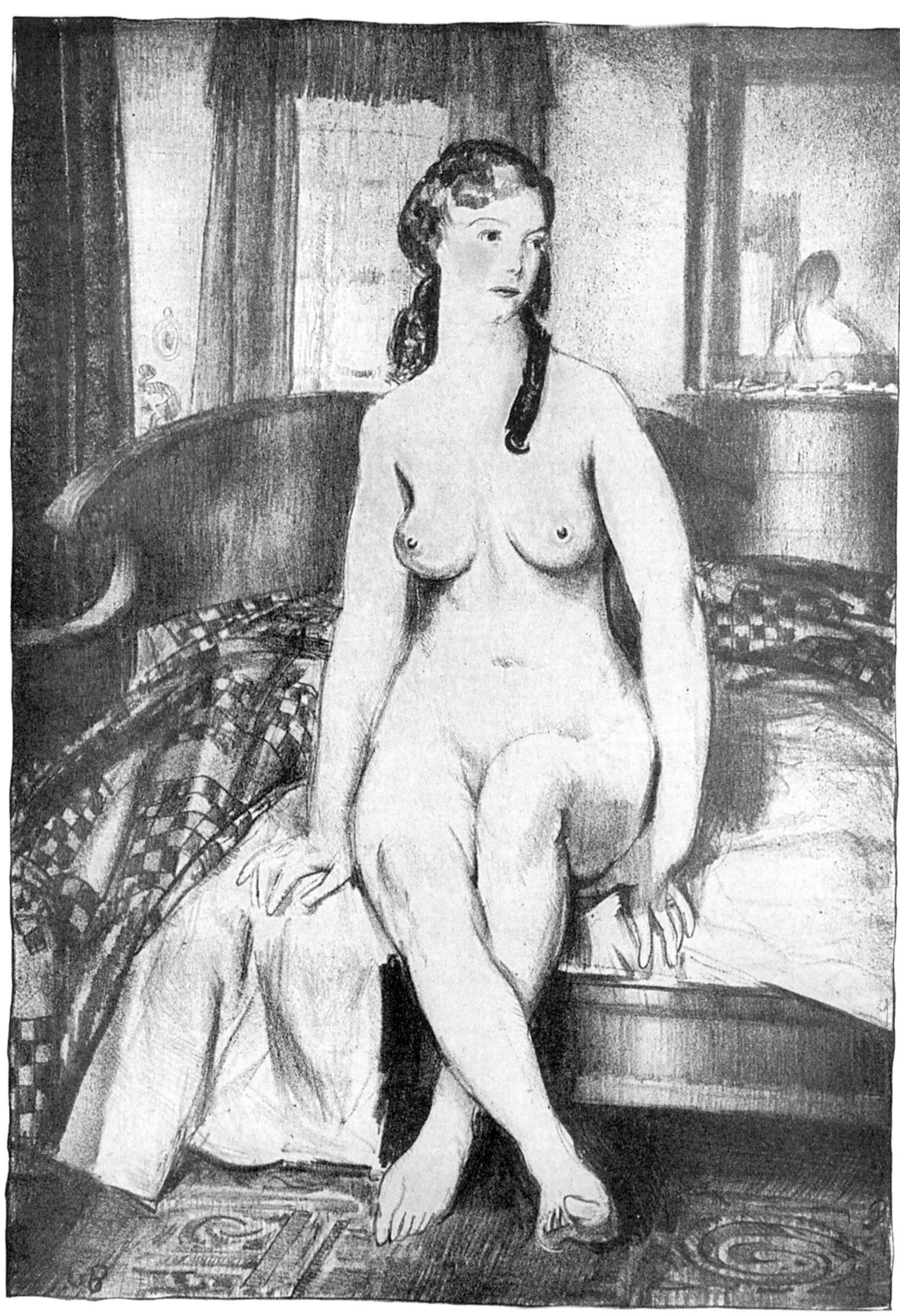

38   Morning, No. 2, Nude

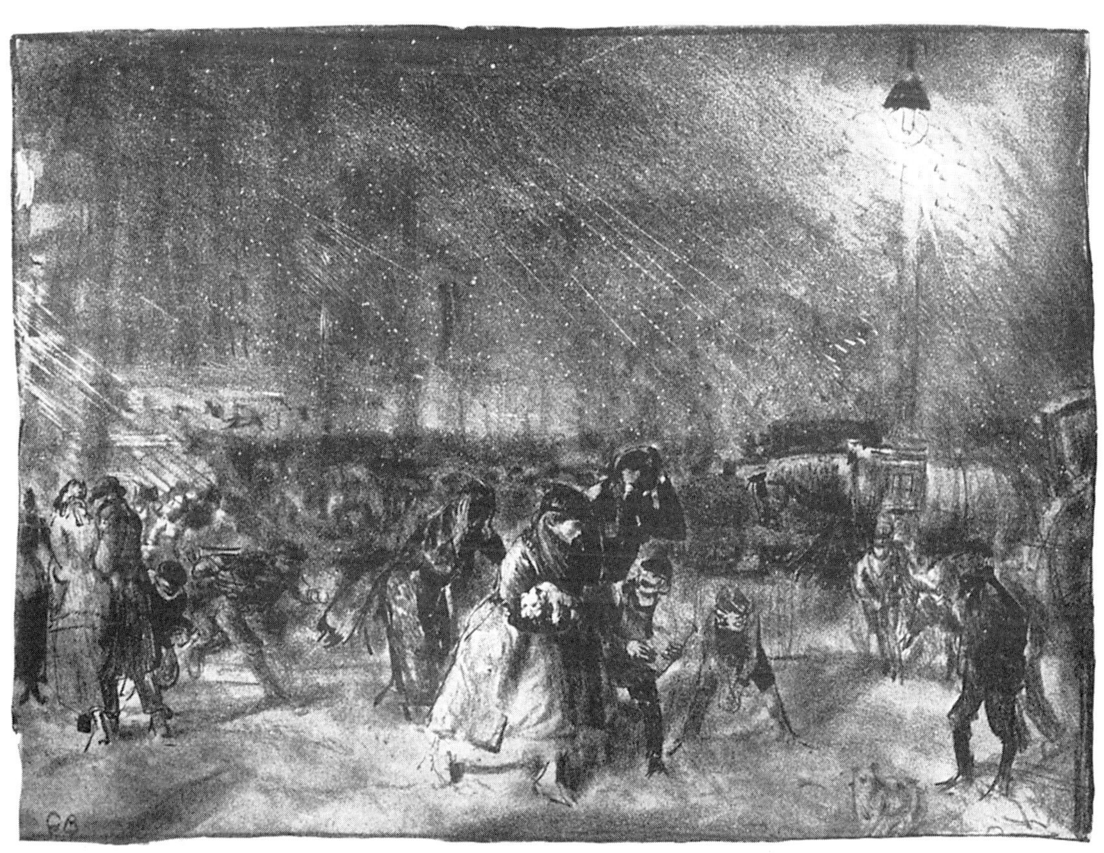

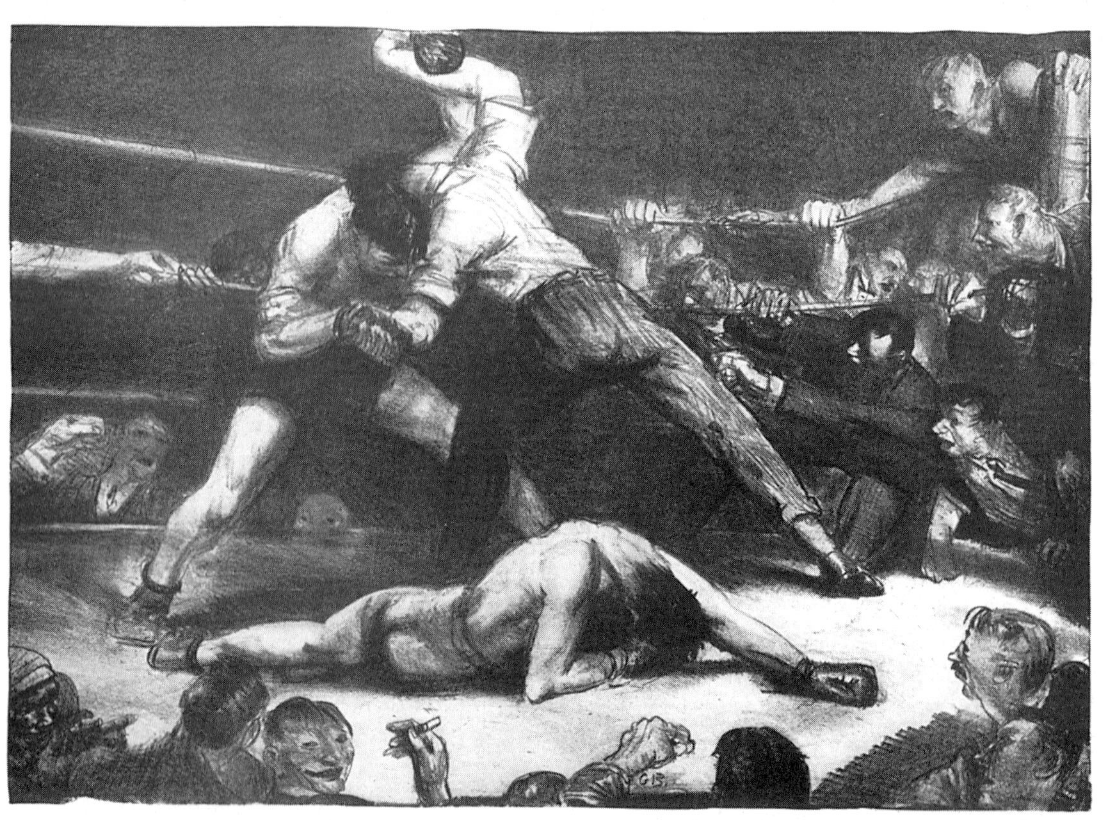

40   *A Knock-out*

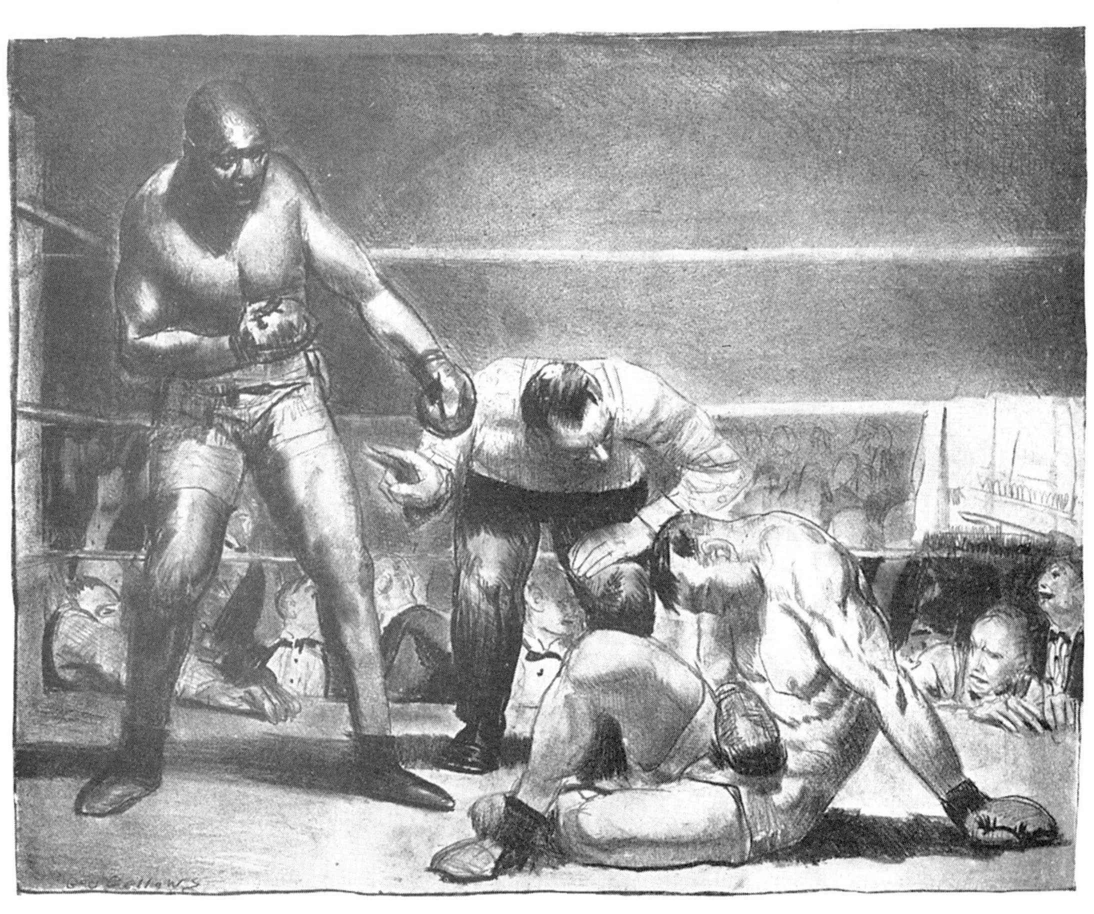

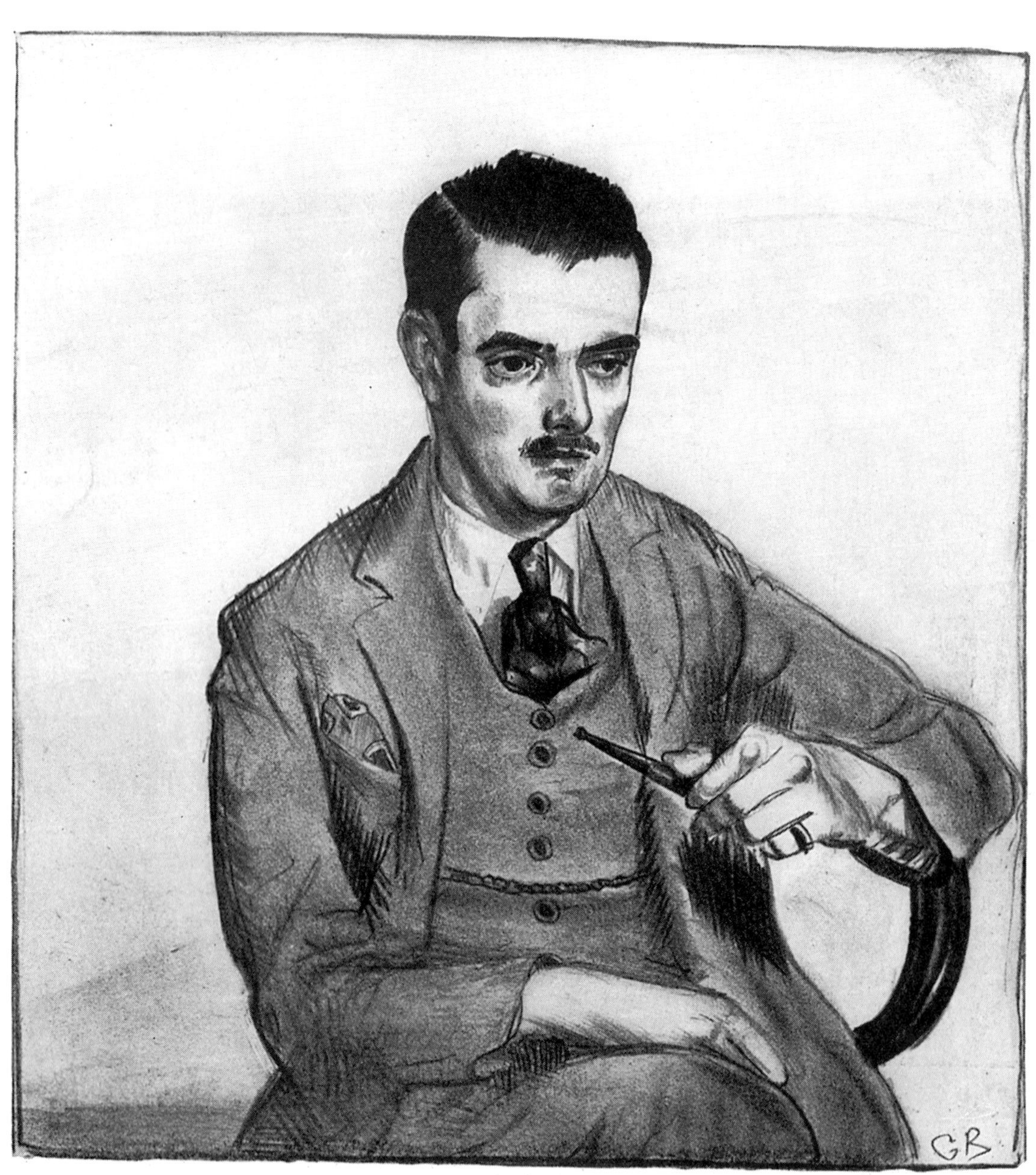

42   *Portrait, Louis Bouché*

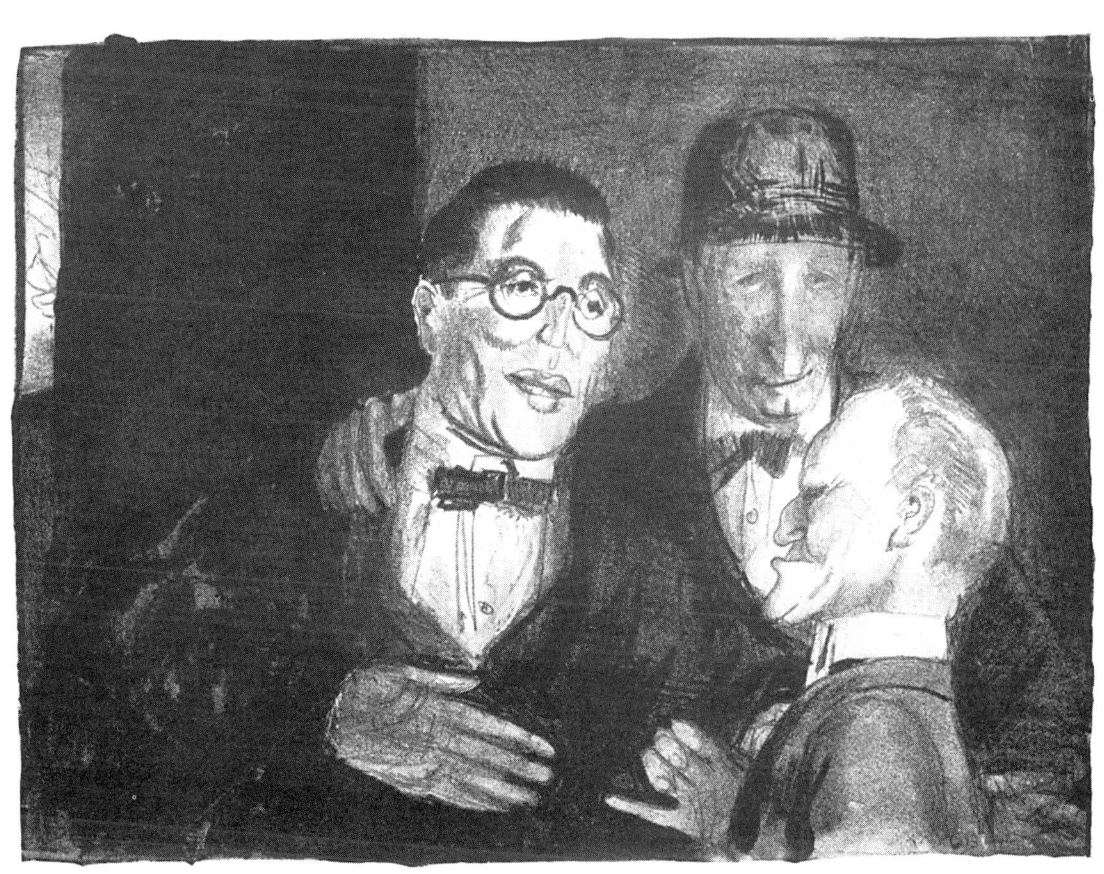

Caricature of Speicher, Kroll and Bellows   43

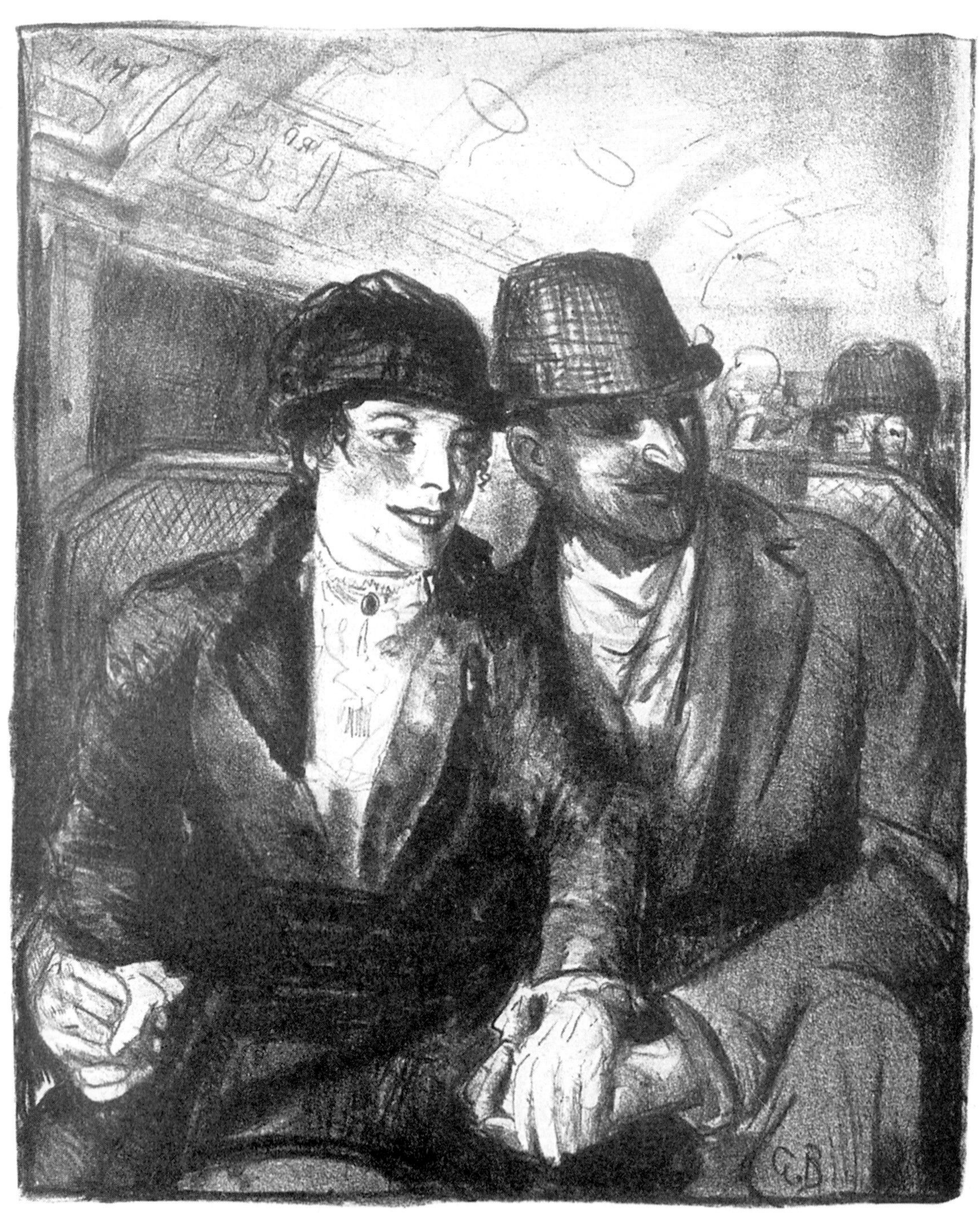

44   *In the Subway*

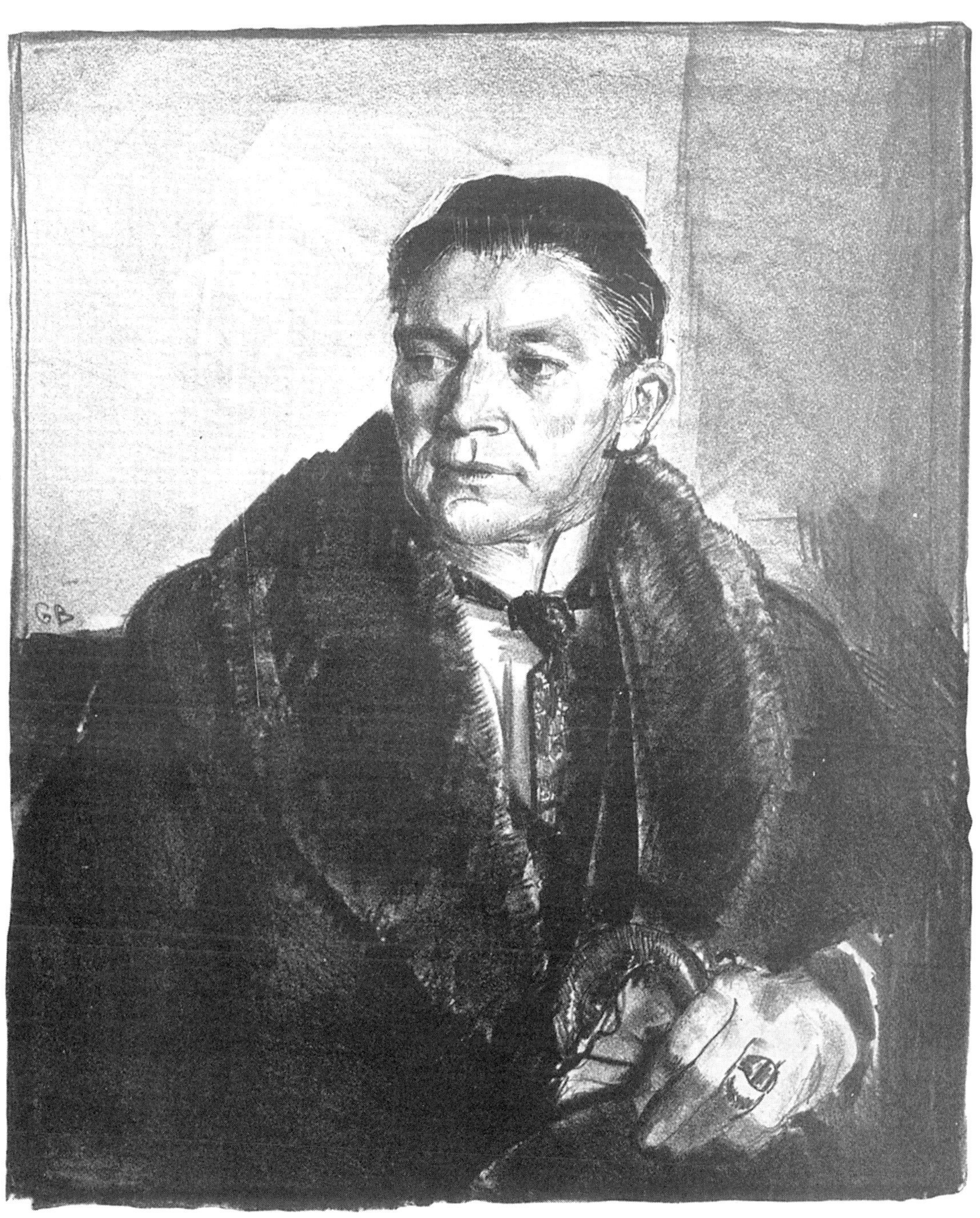

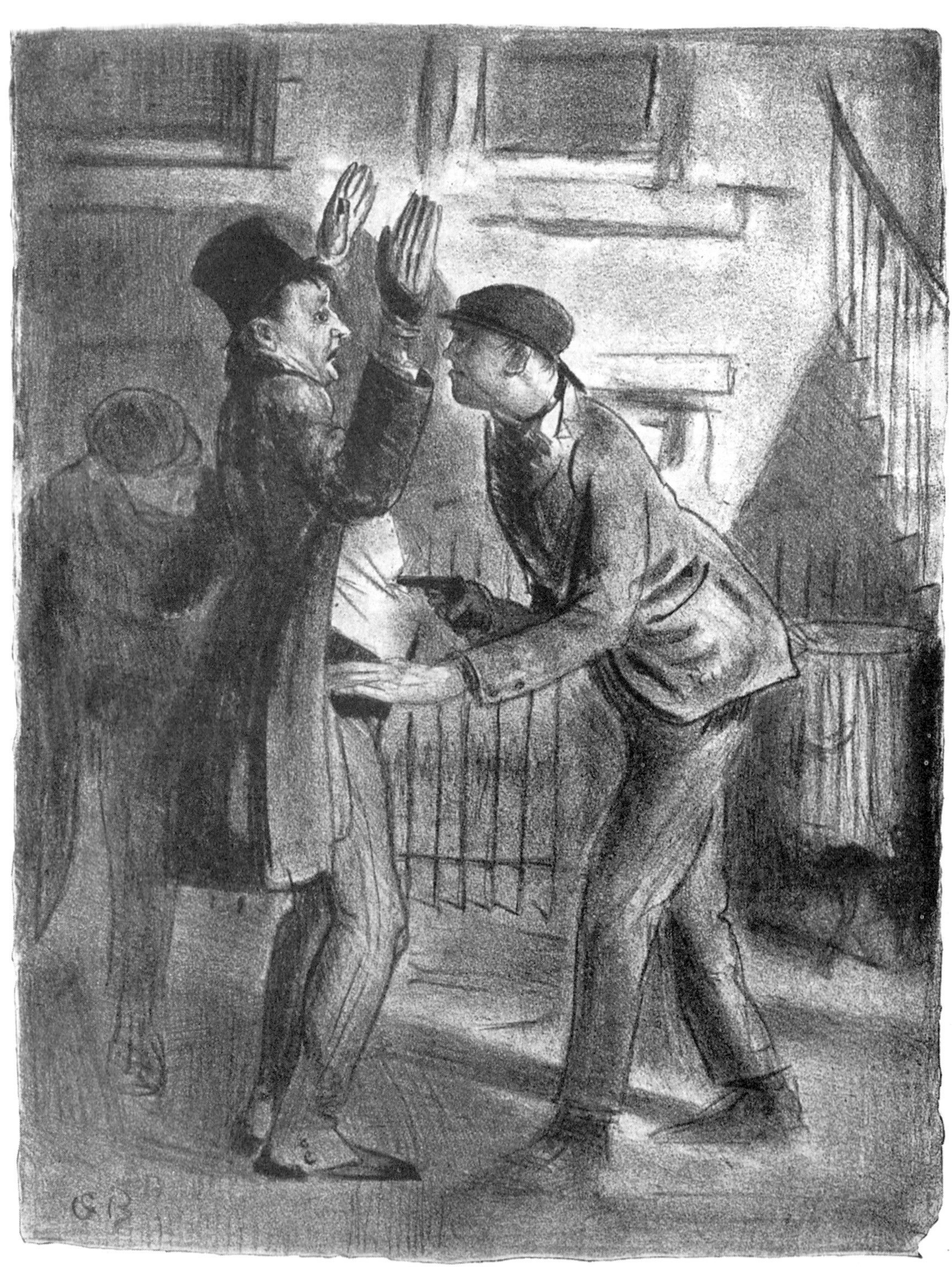

46   *The Hold-up, First State*

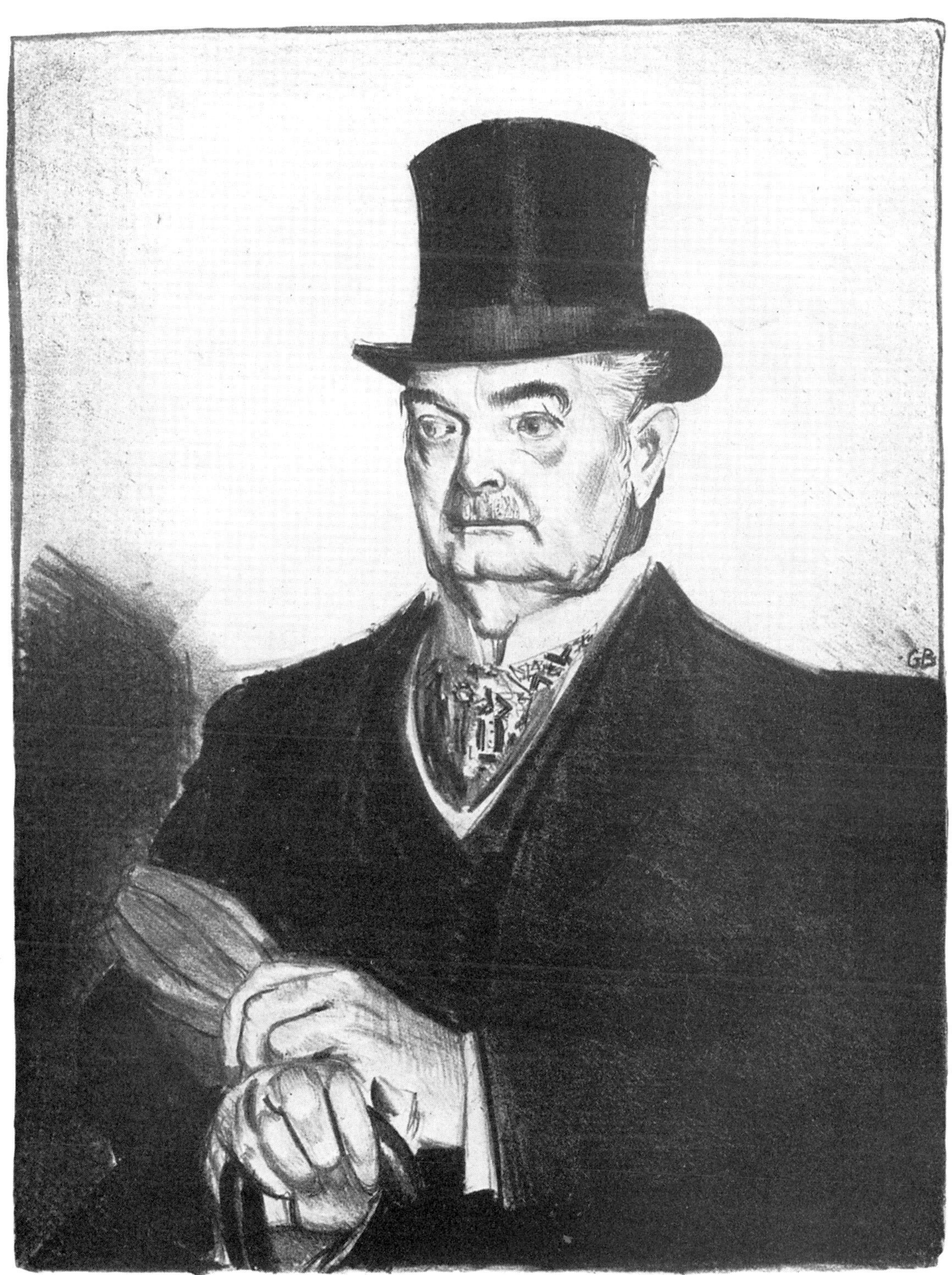

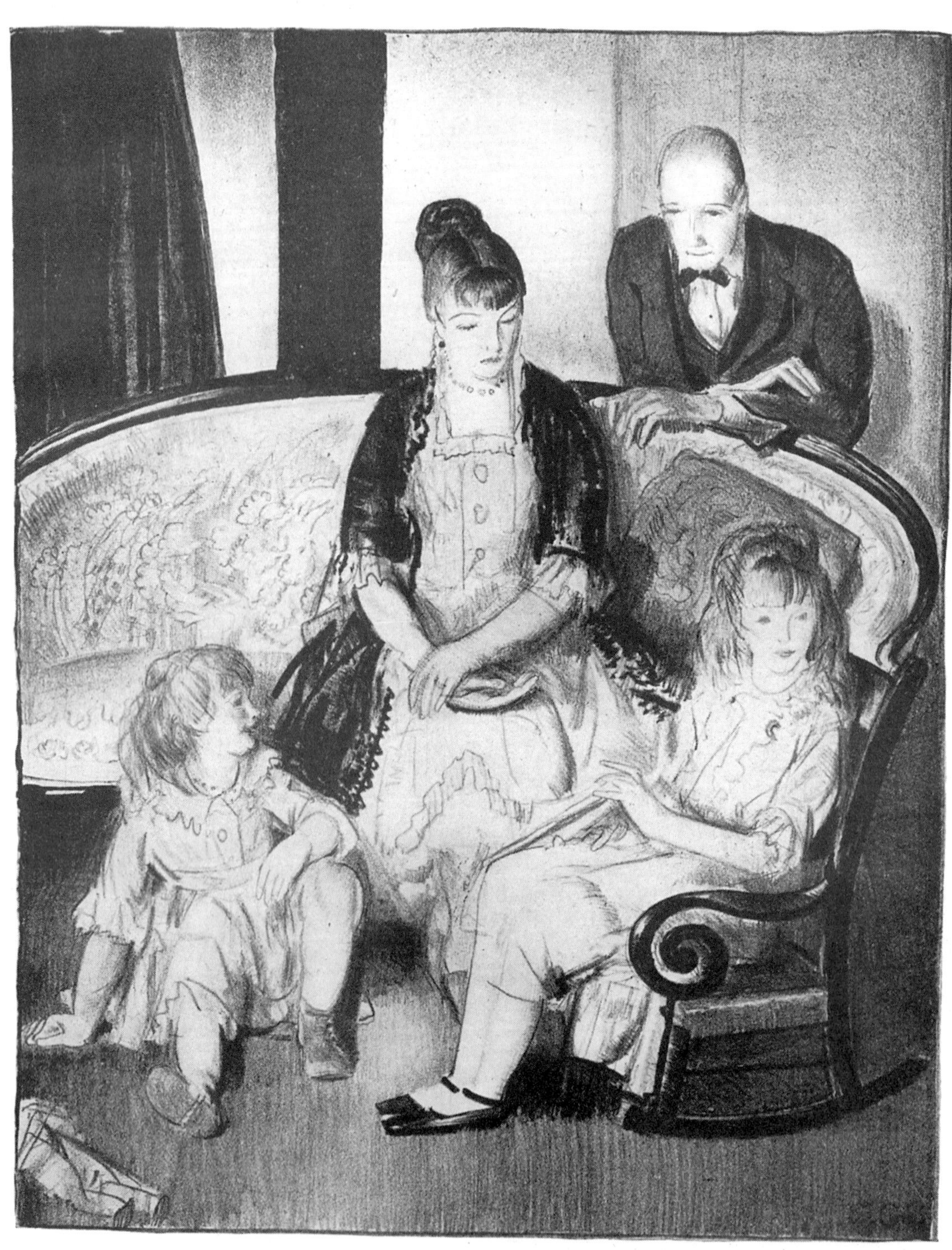

48   *My Family, No. 2*

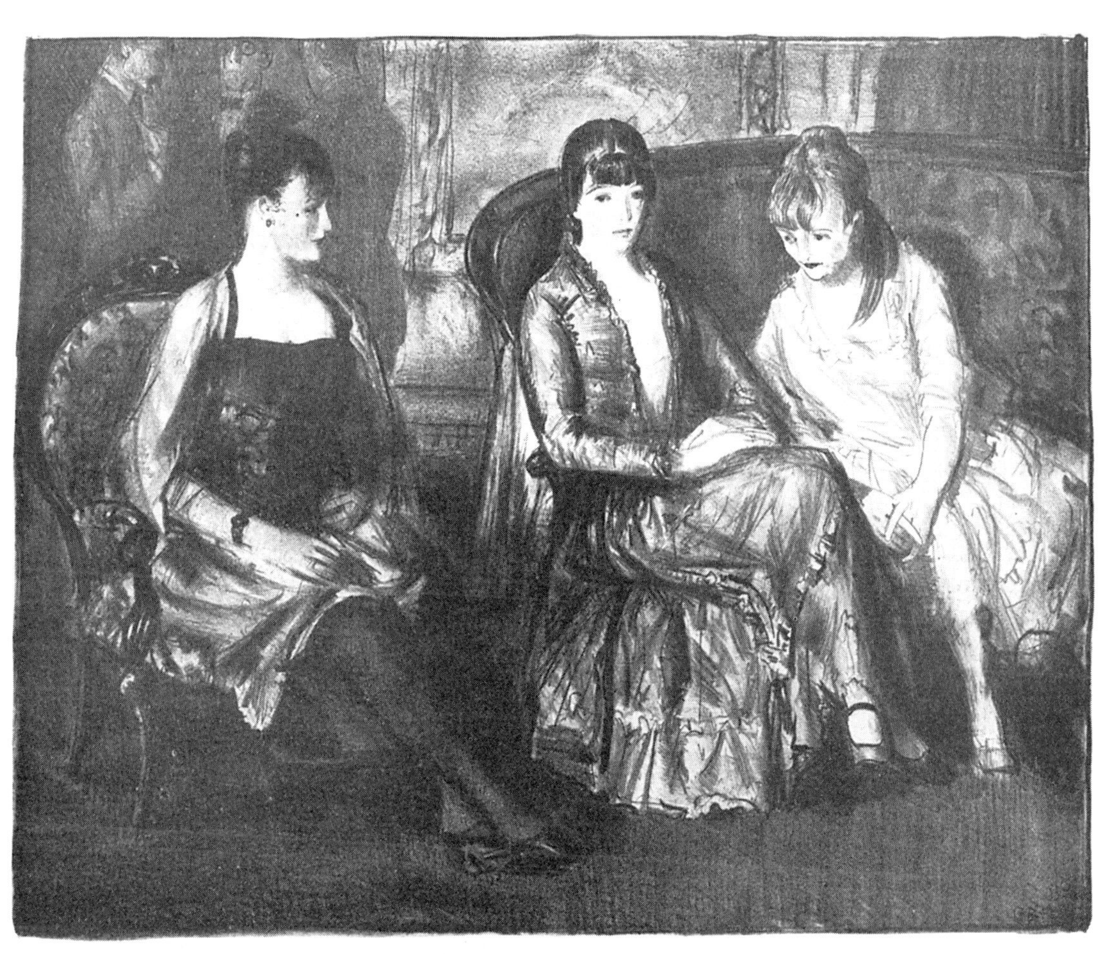

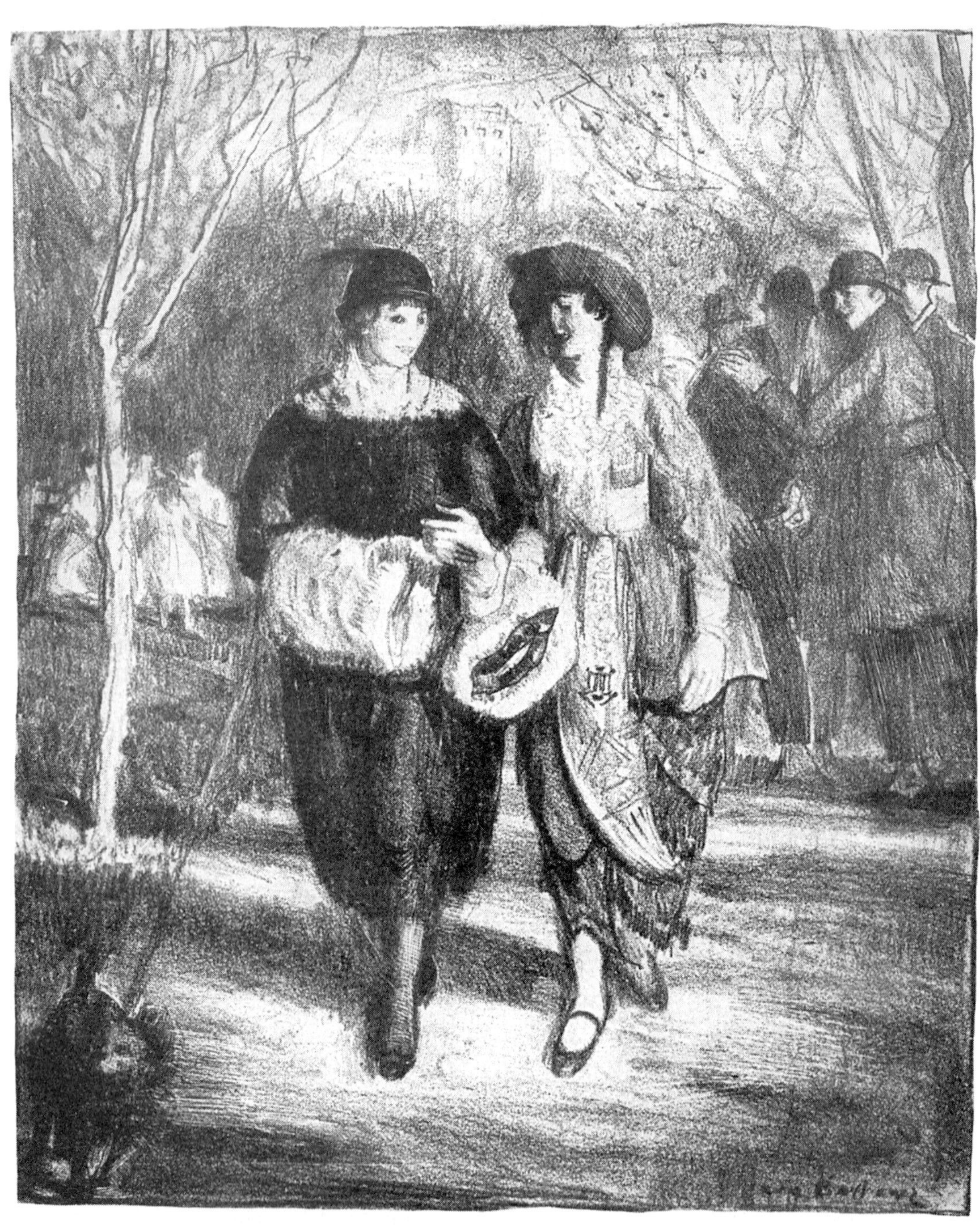

50 *Spring, Central Park*

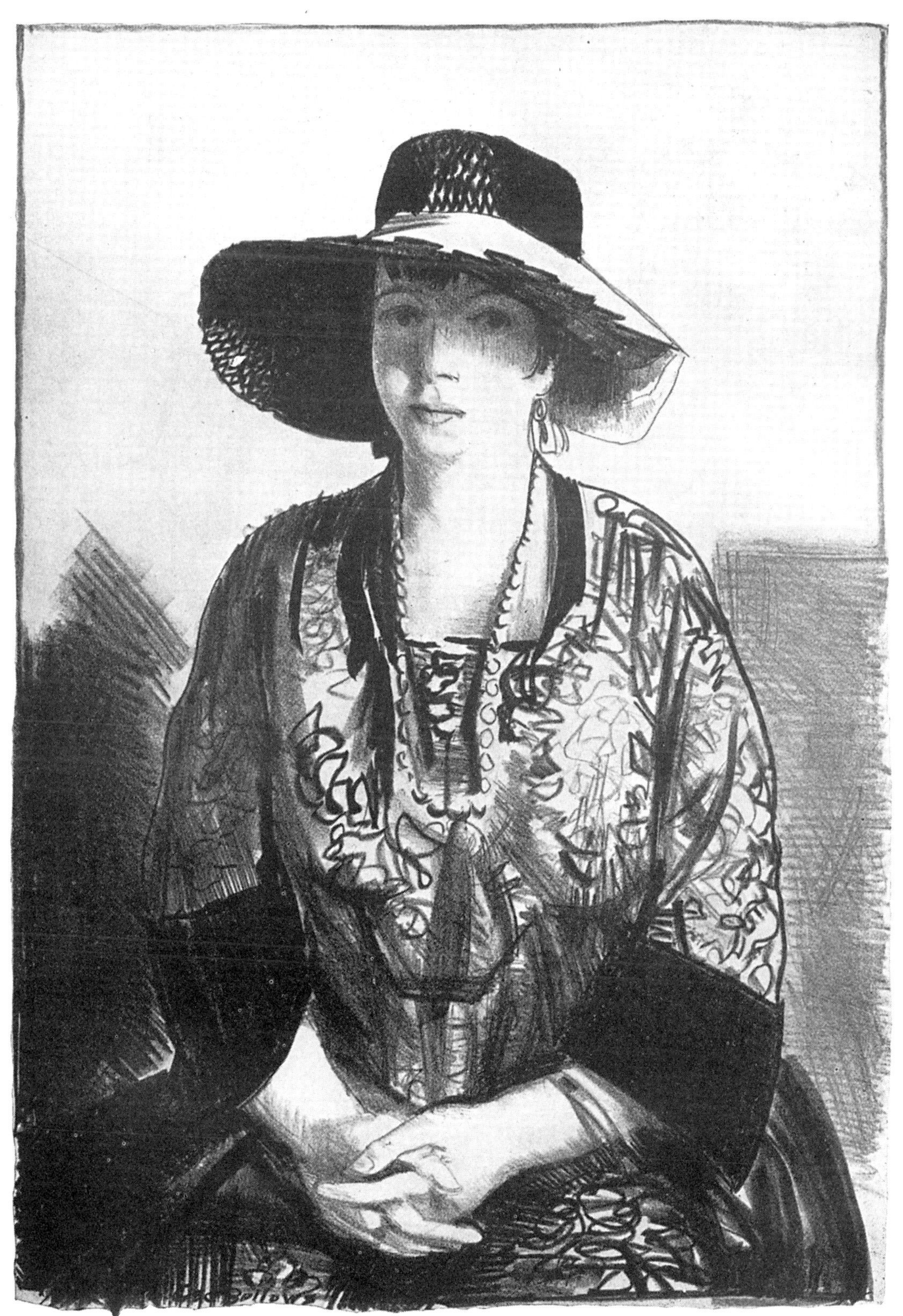

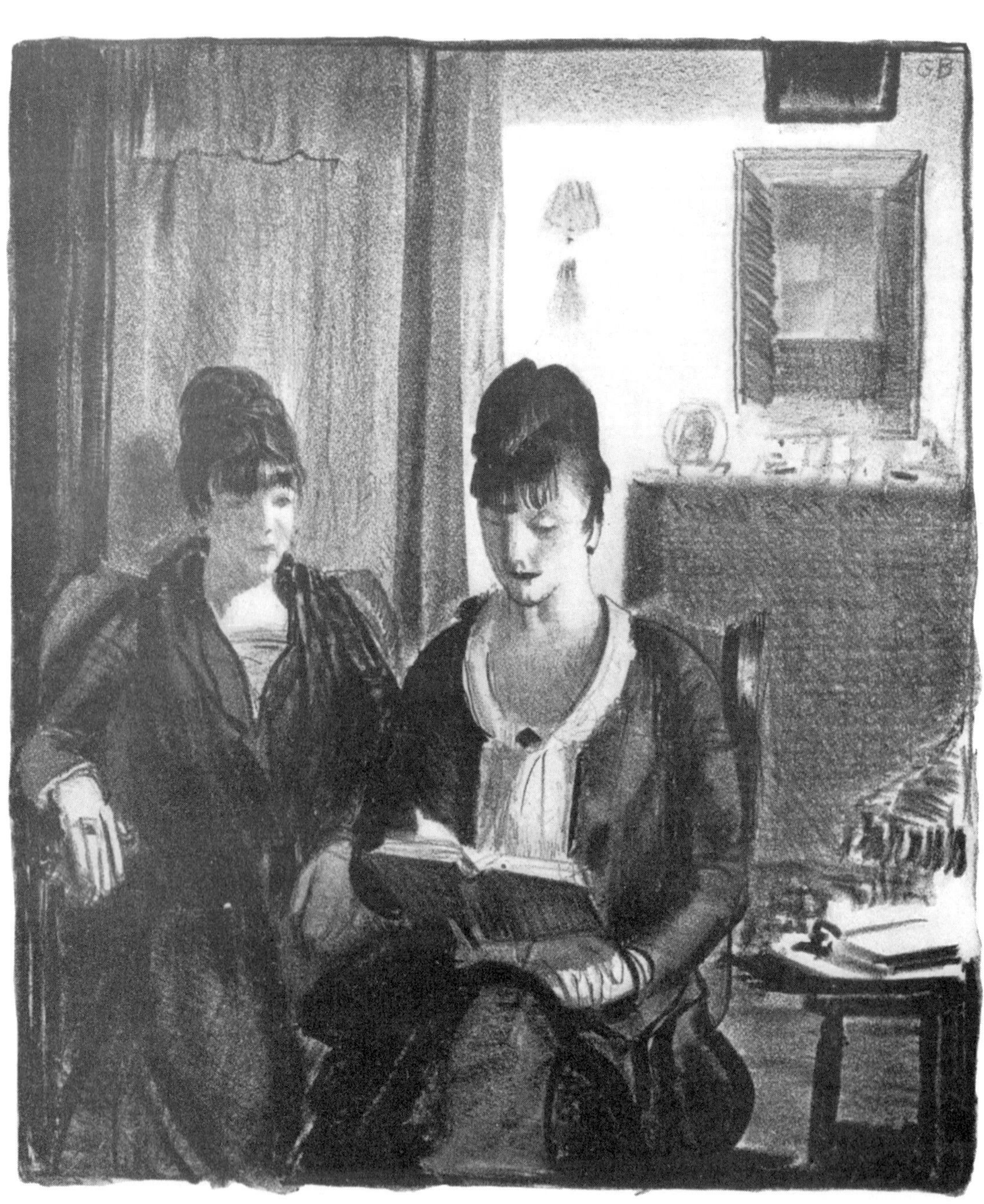

52 *Elsie Reading to Emma, First State*

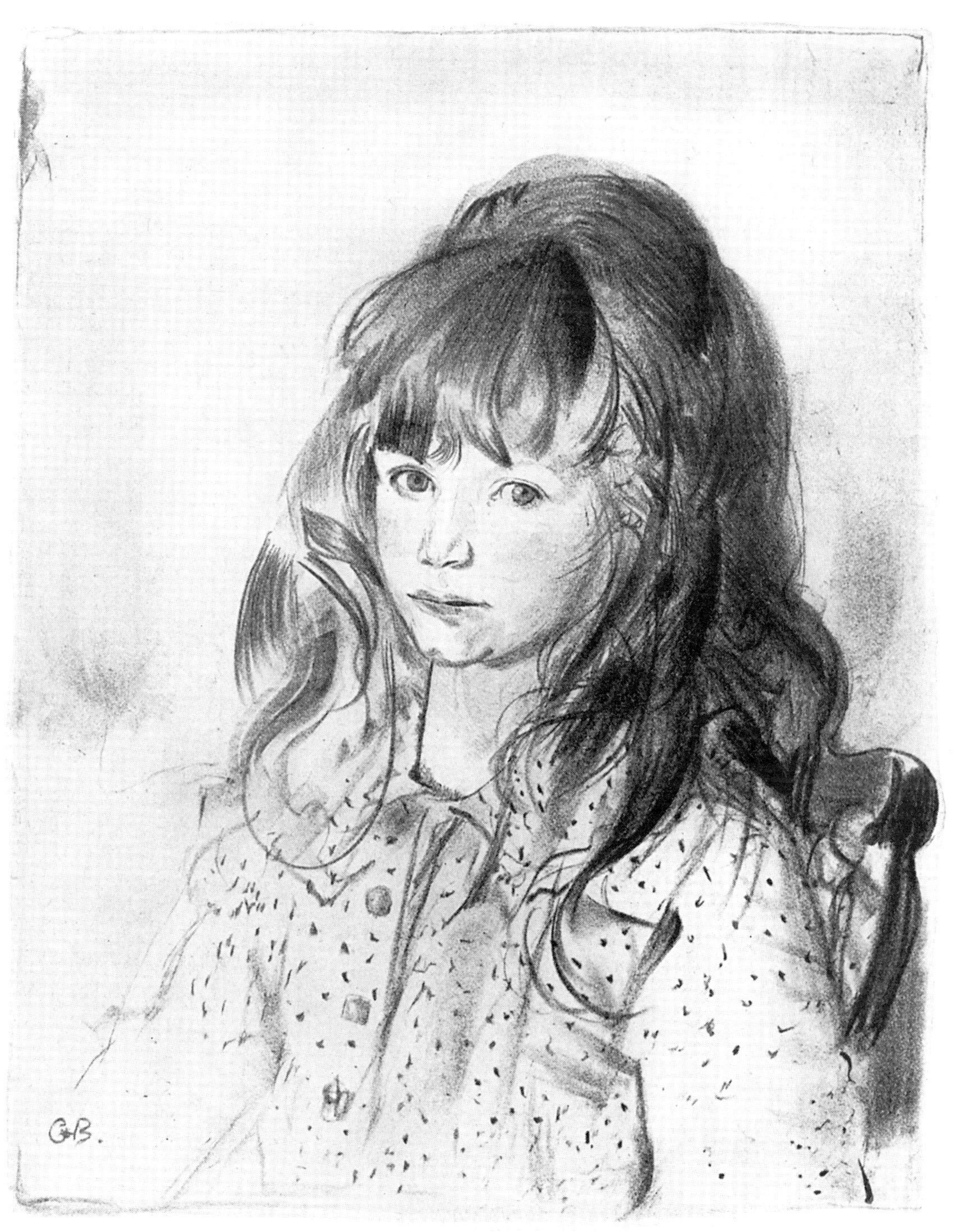

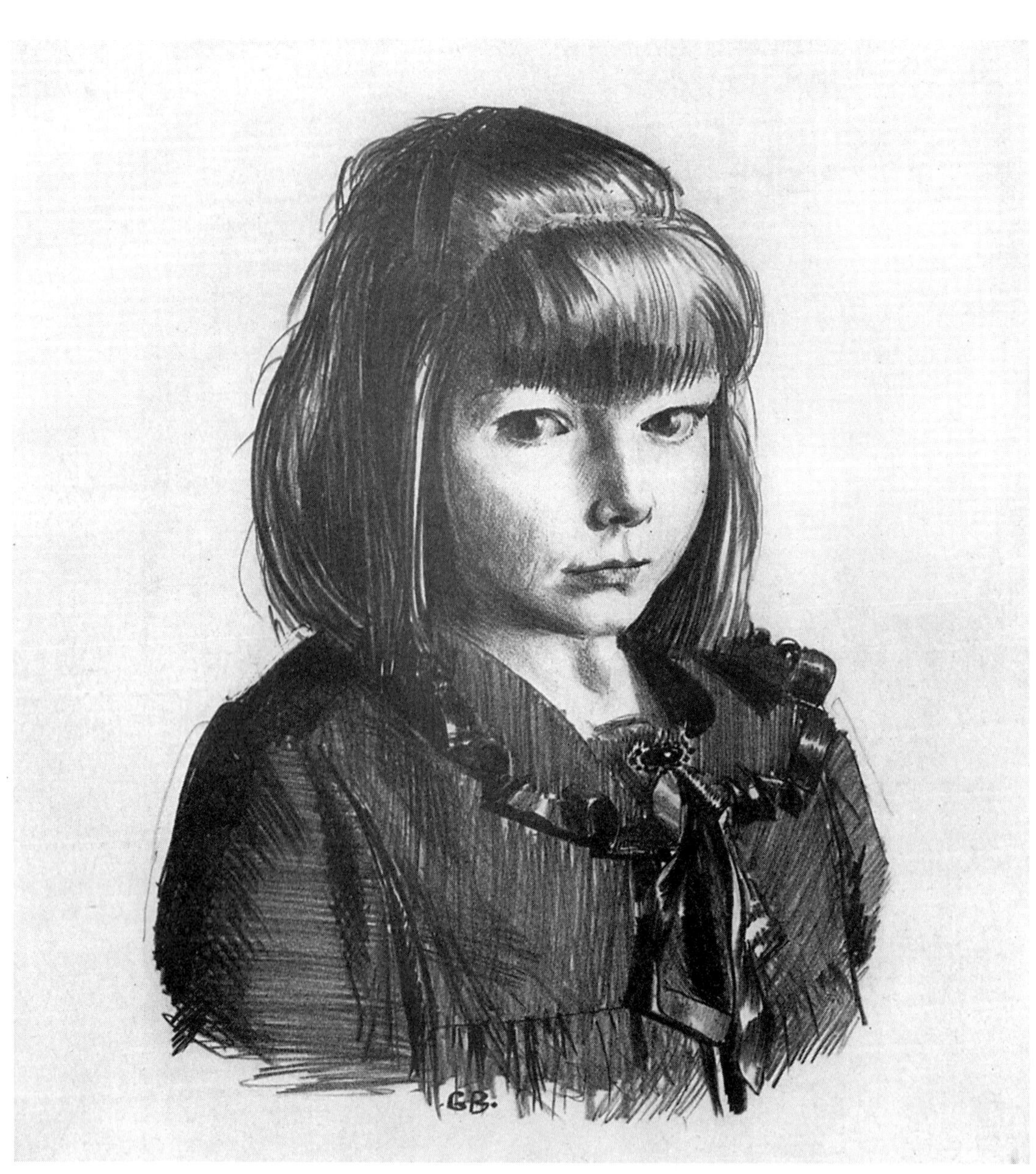

54 *Jean*

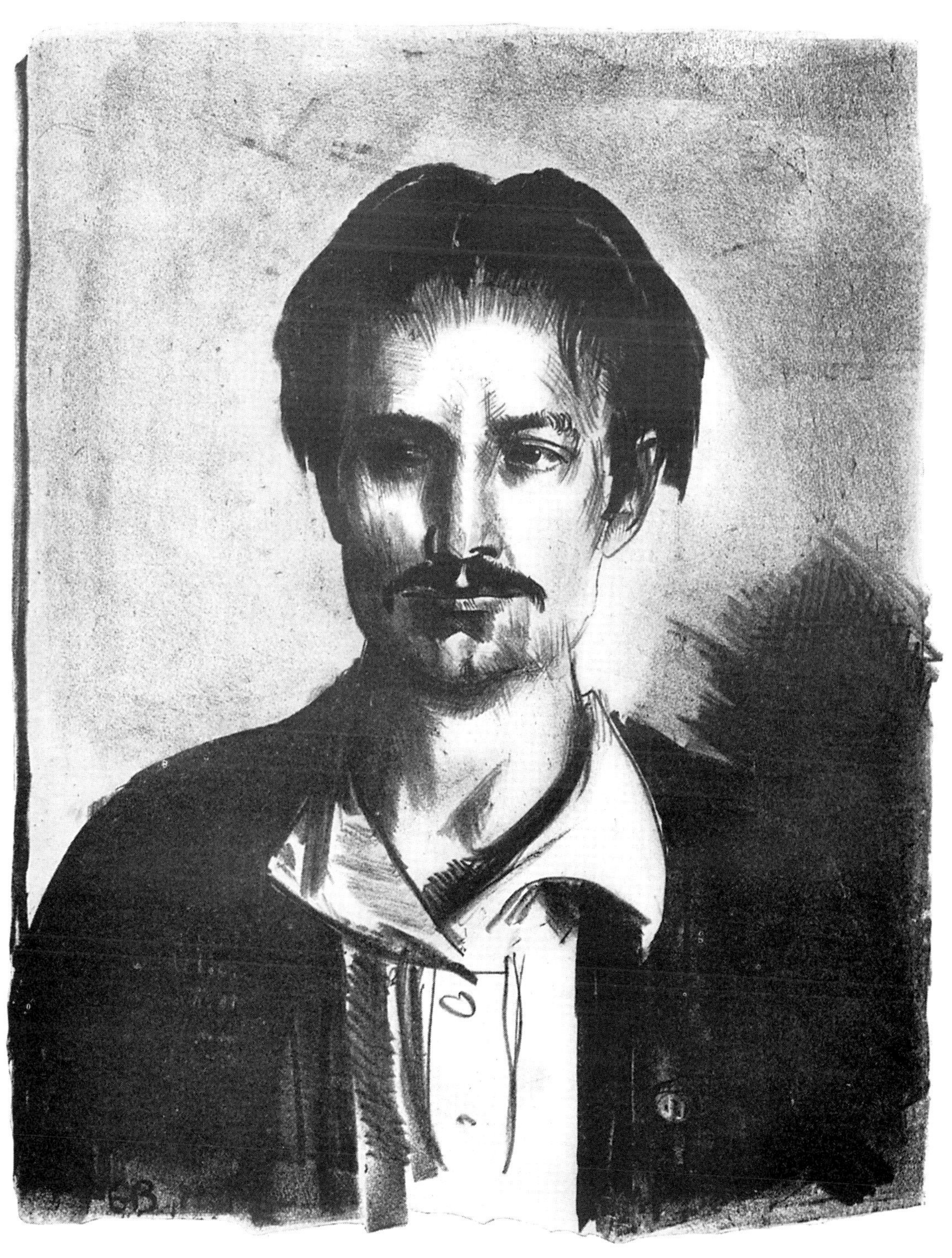

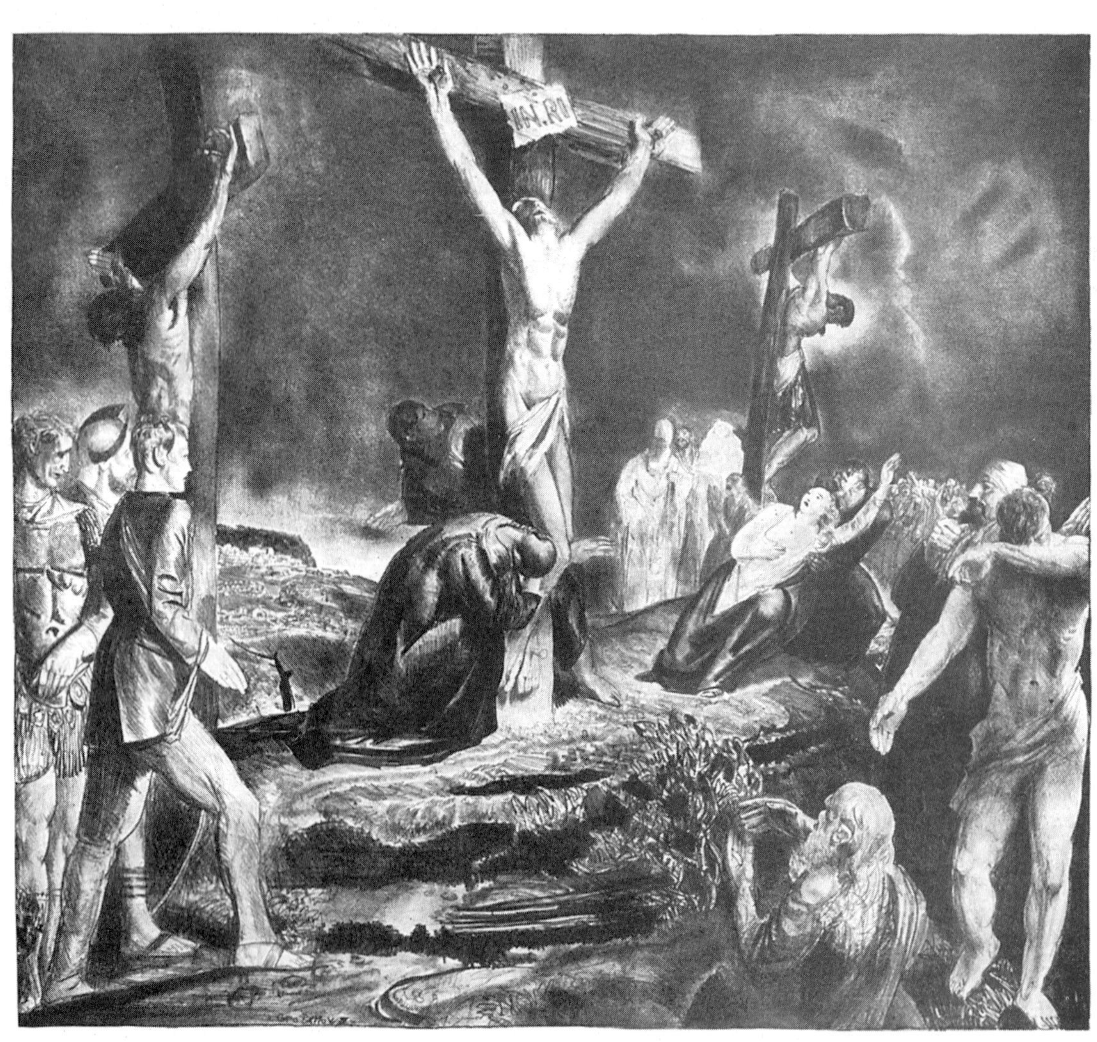

56 *Crucifixion of Christ*

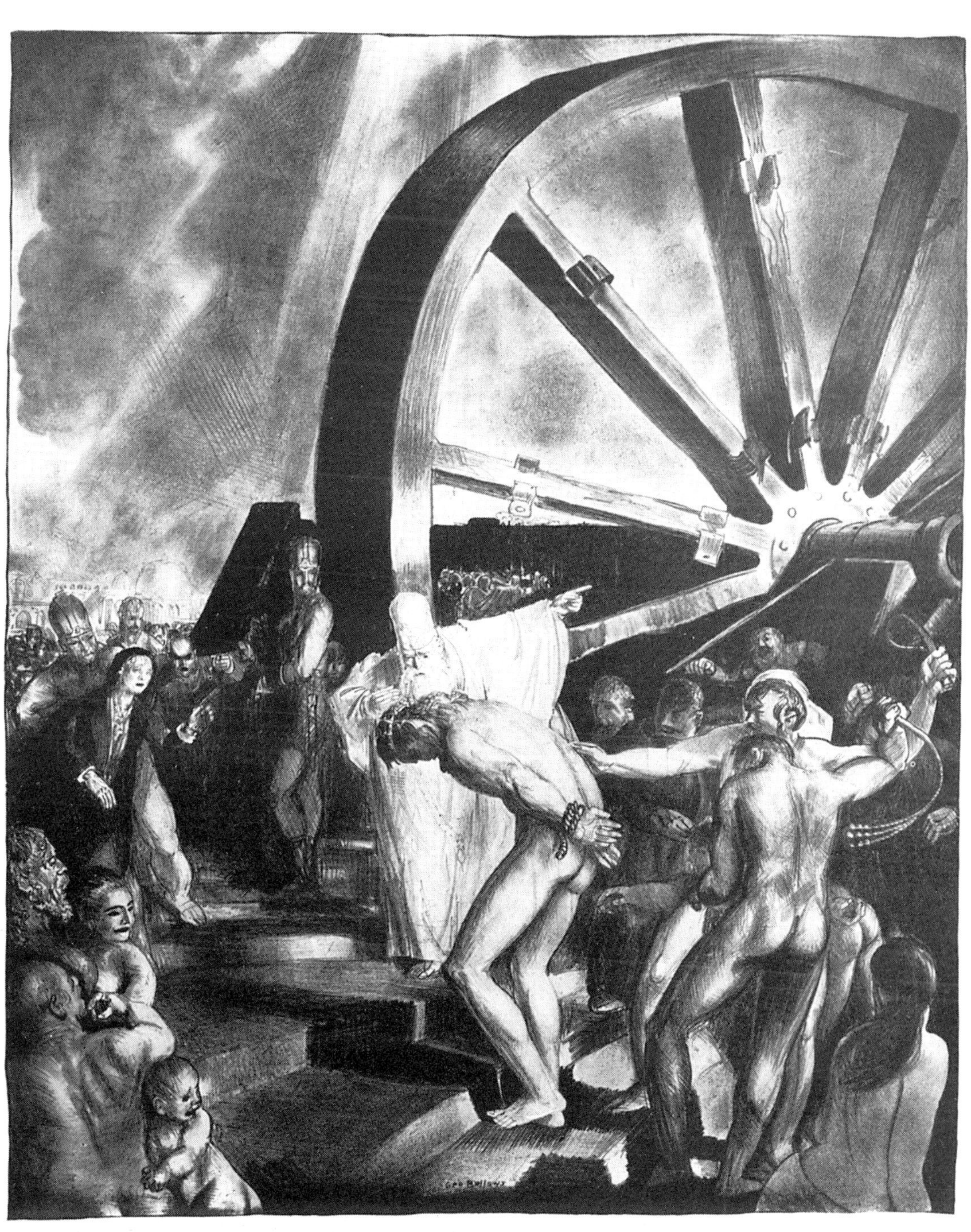

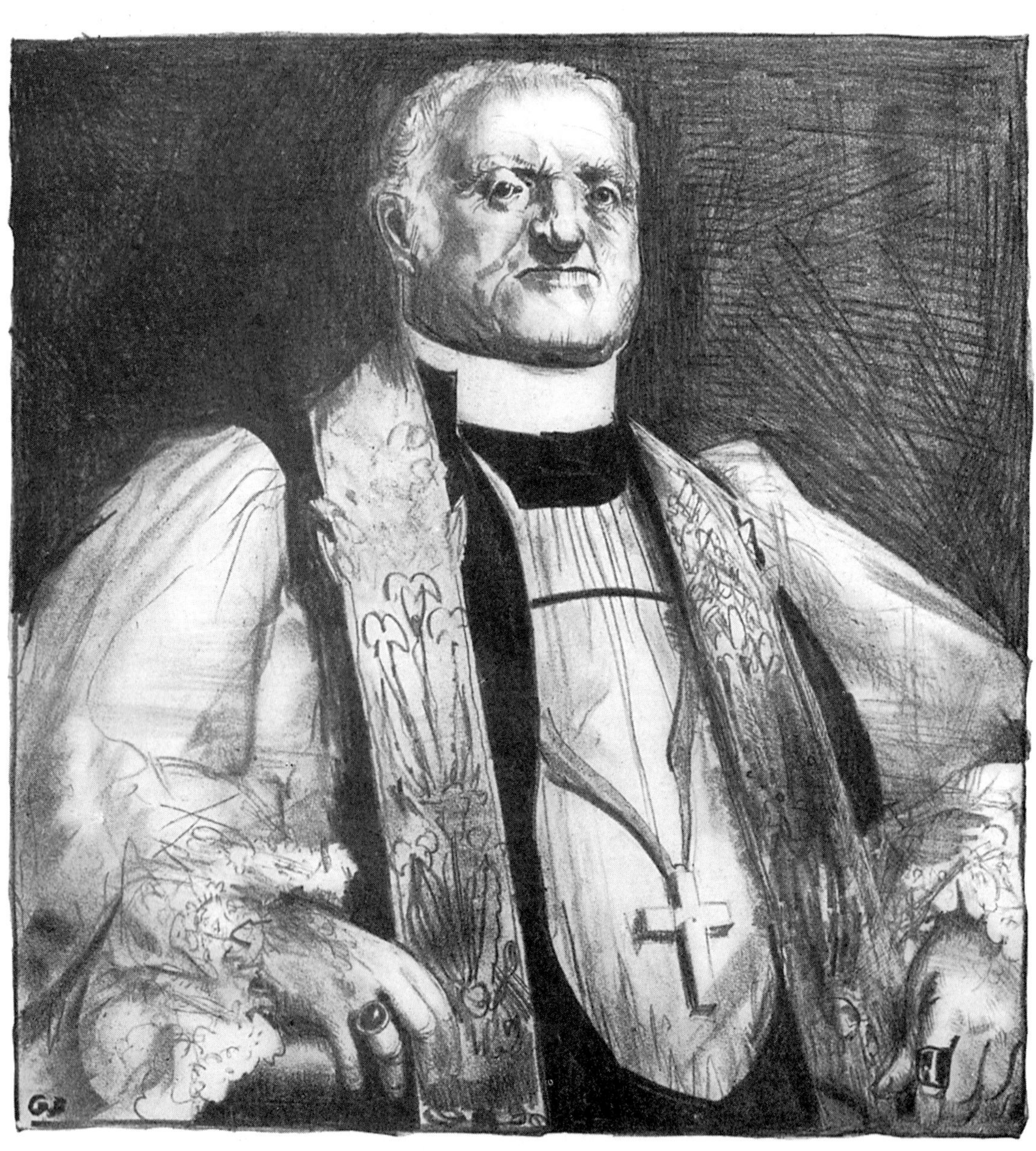

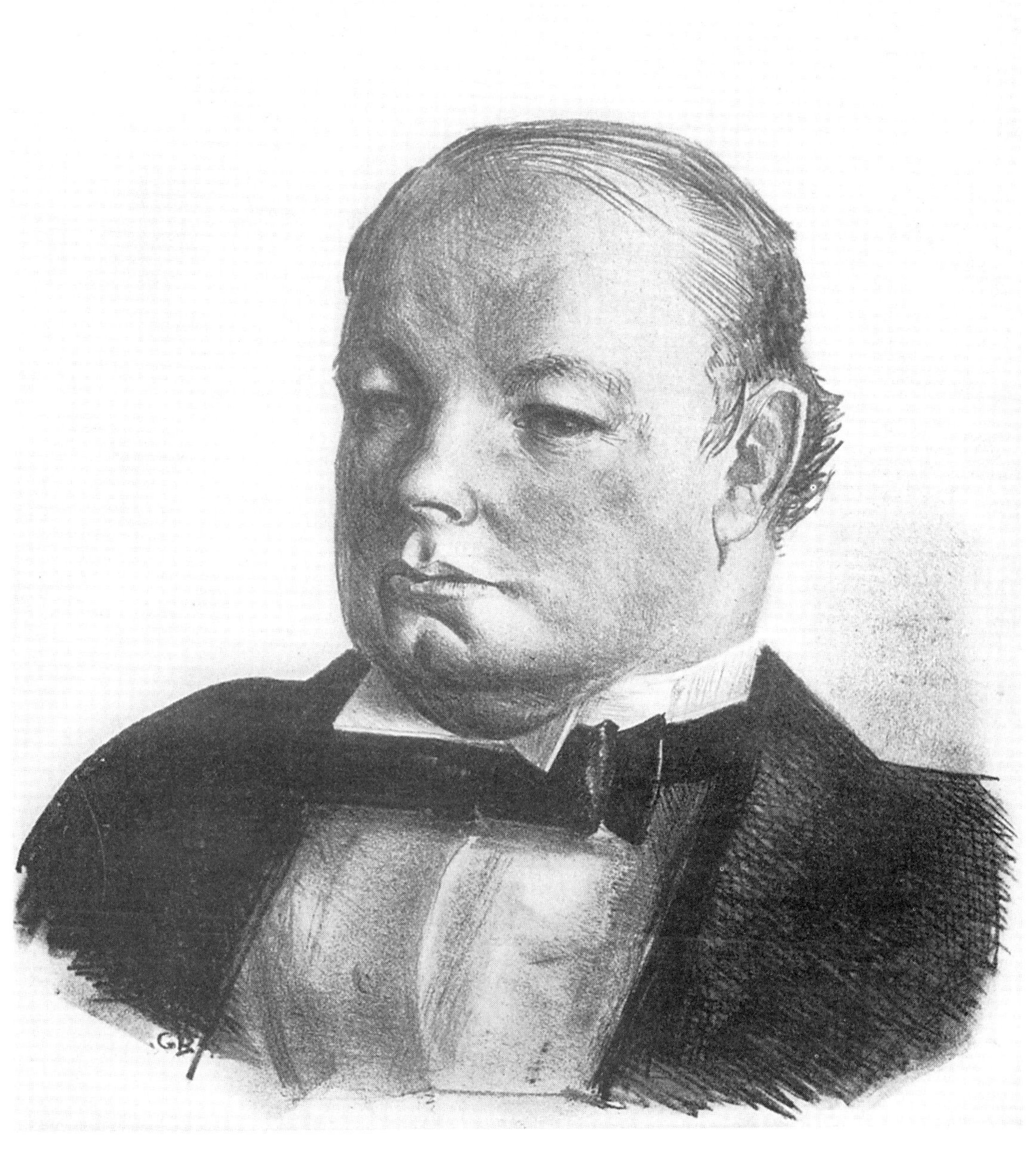

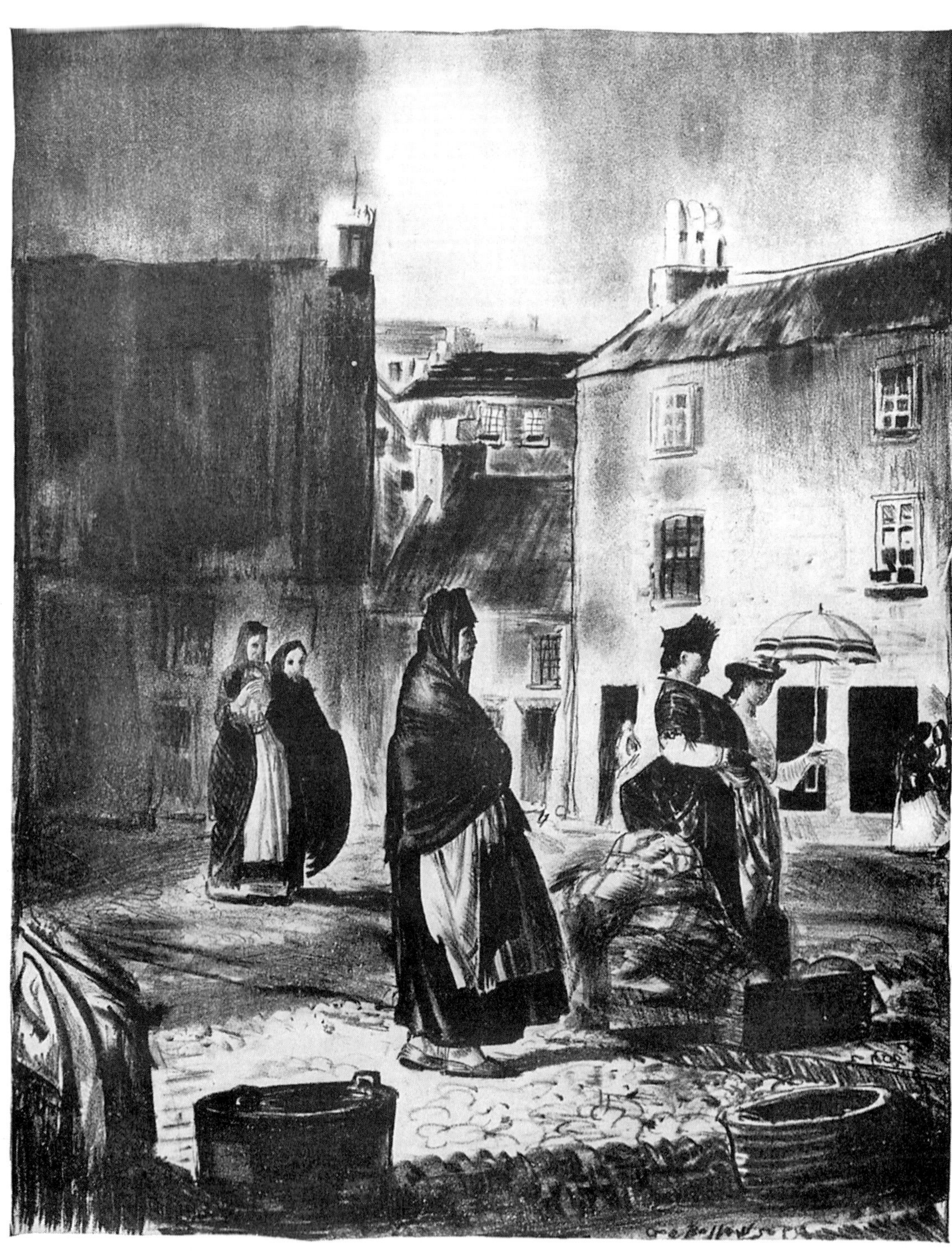

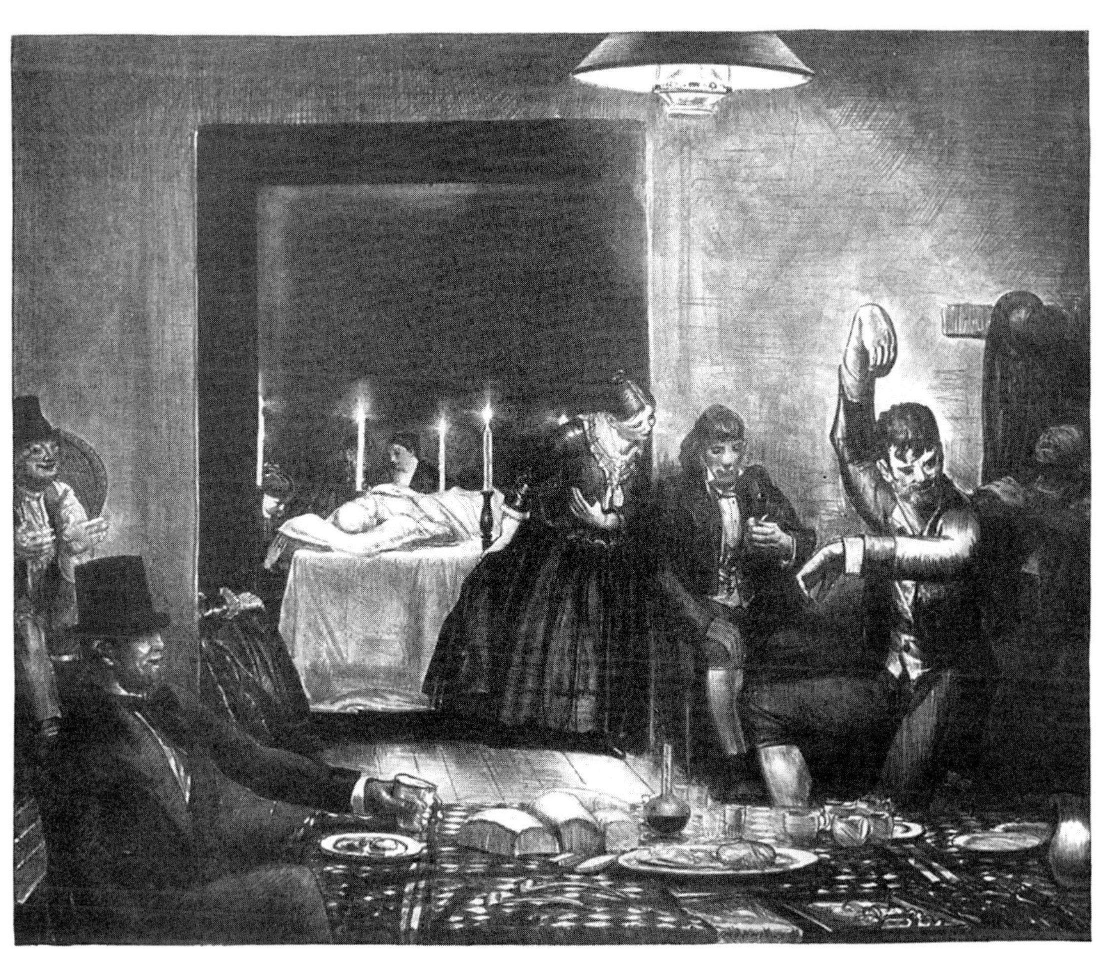

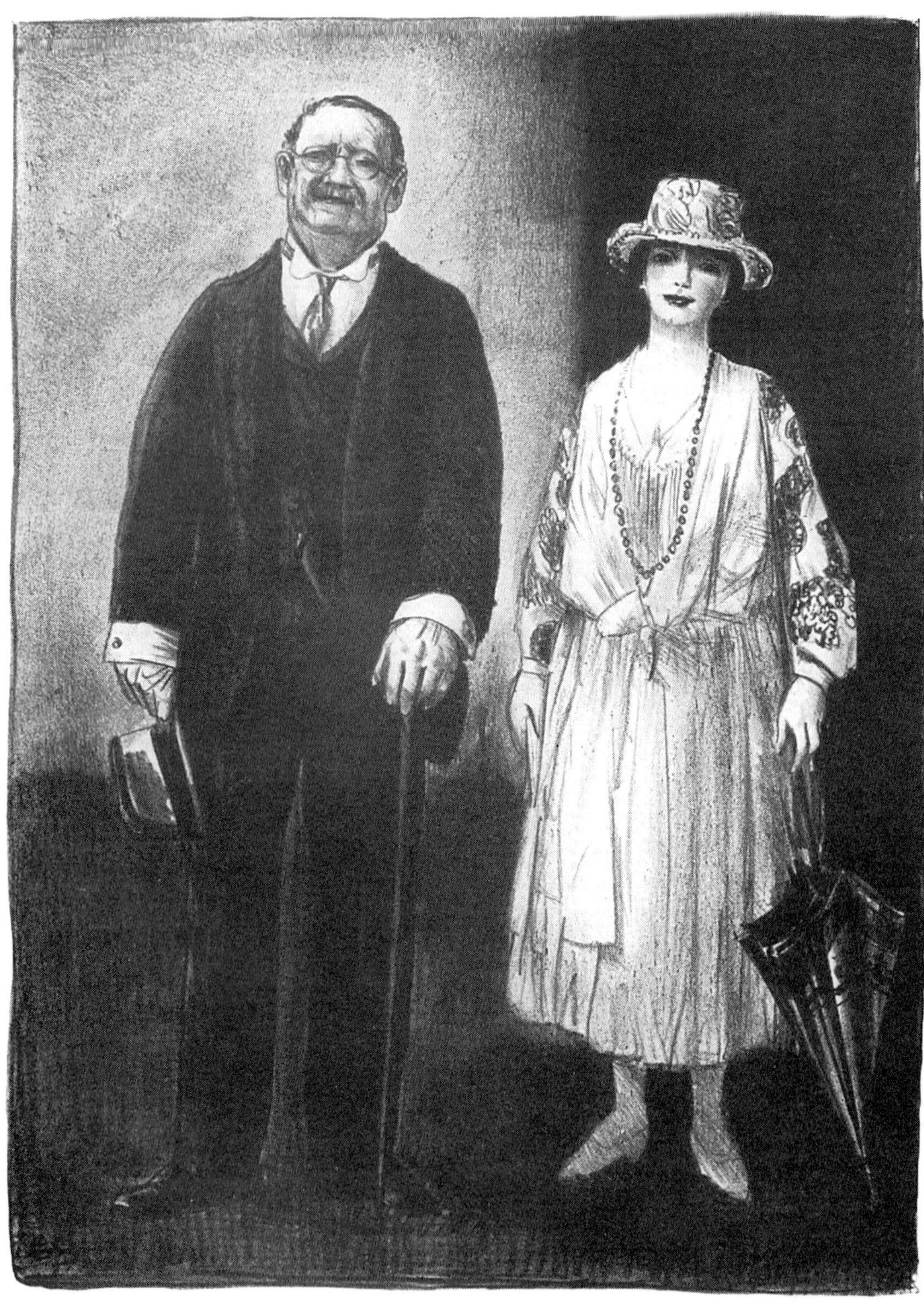

62 *Married Couple*

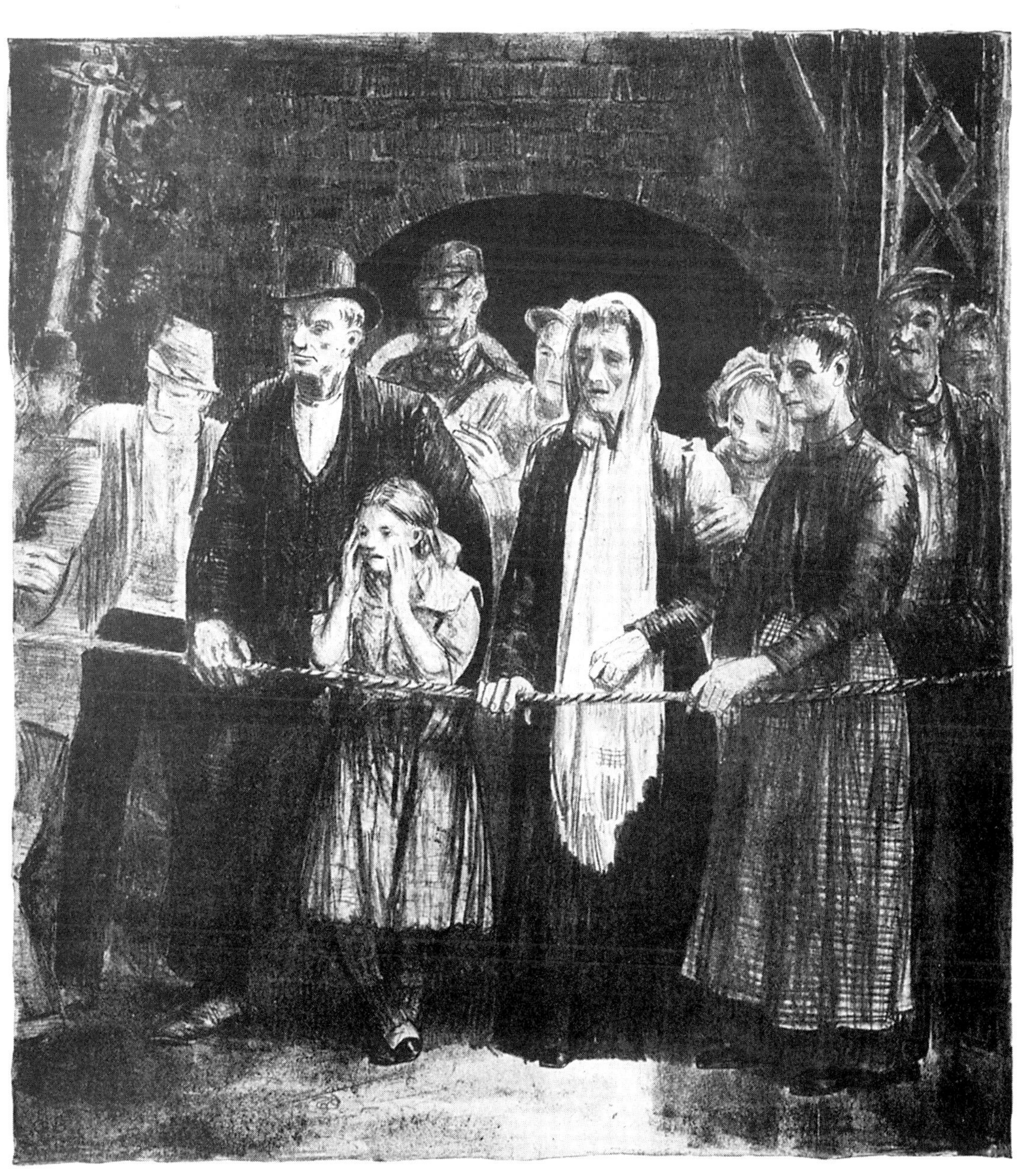

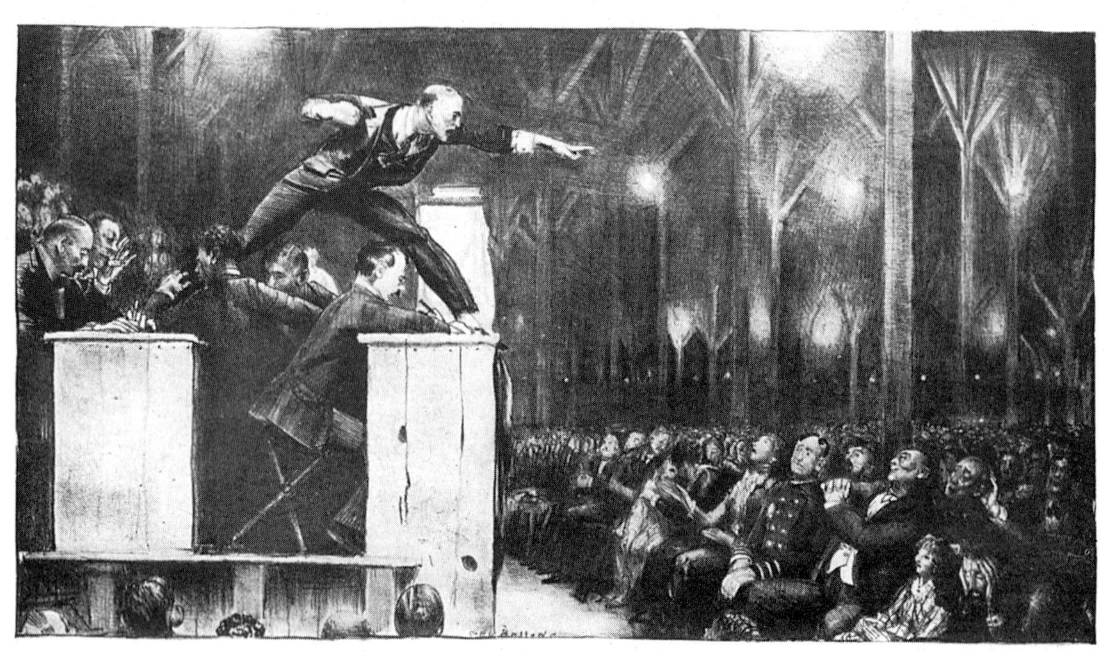

64   *Billy Sunday*

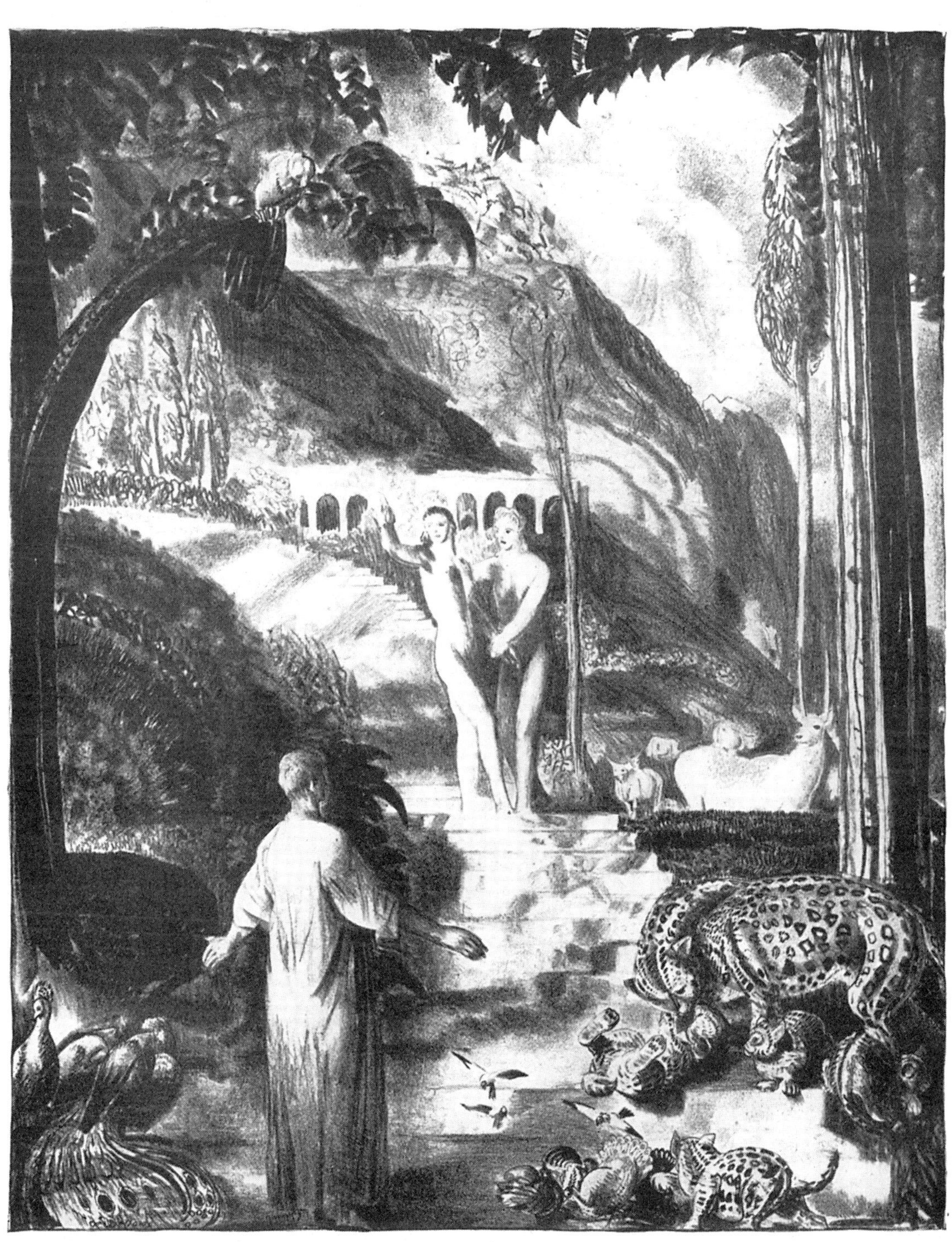

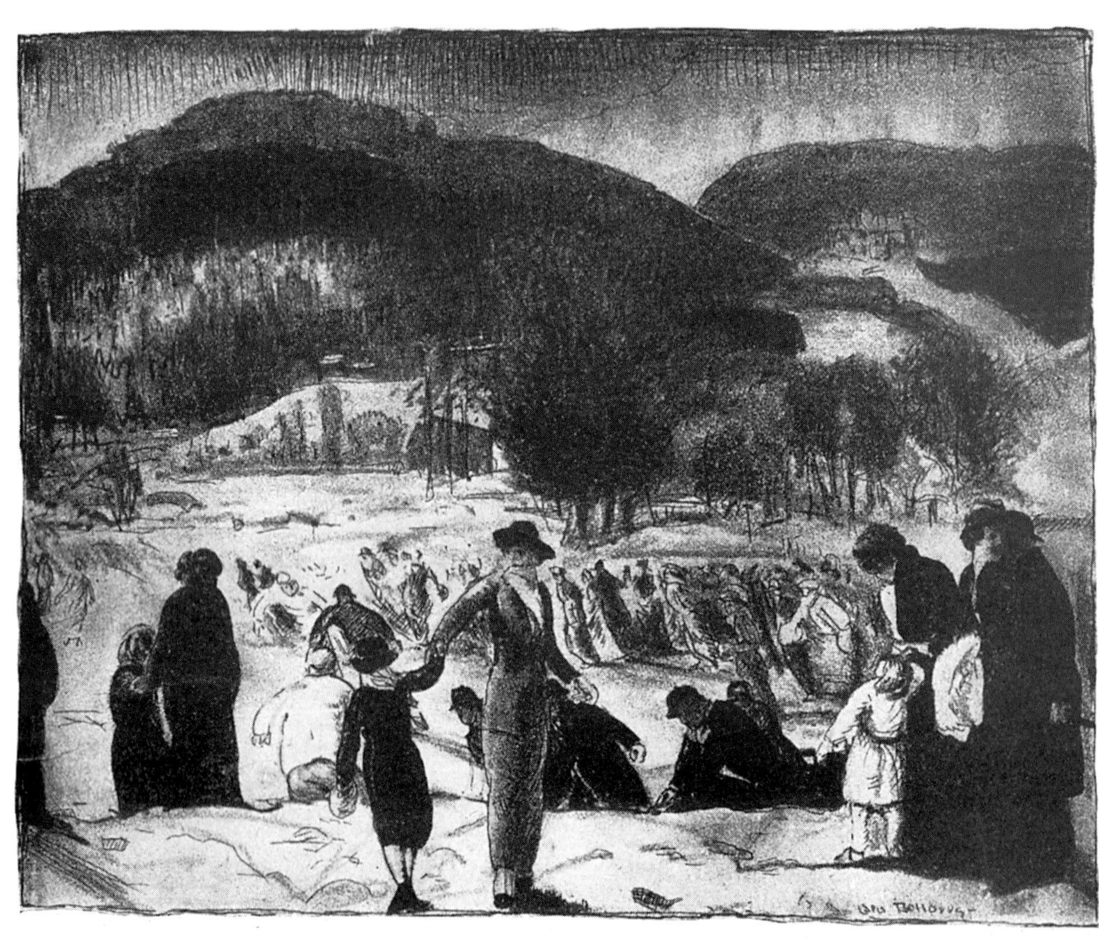

66   *Love of Winter*

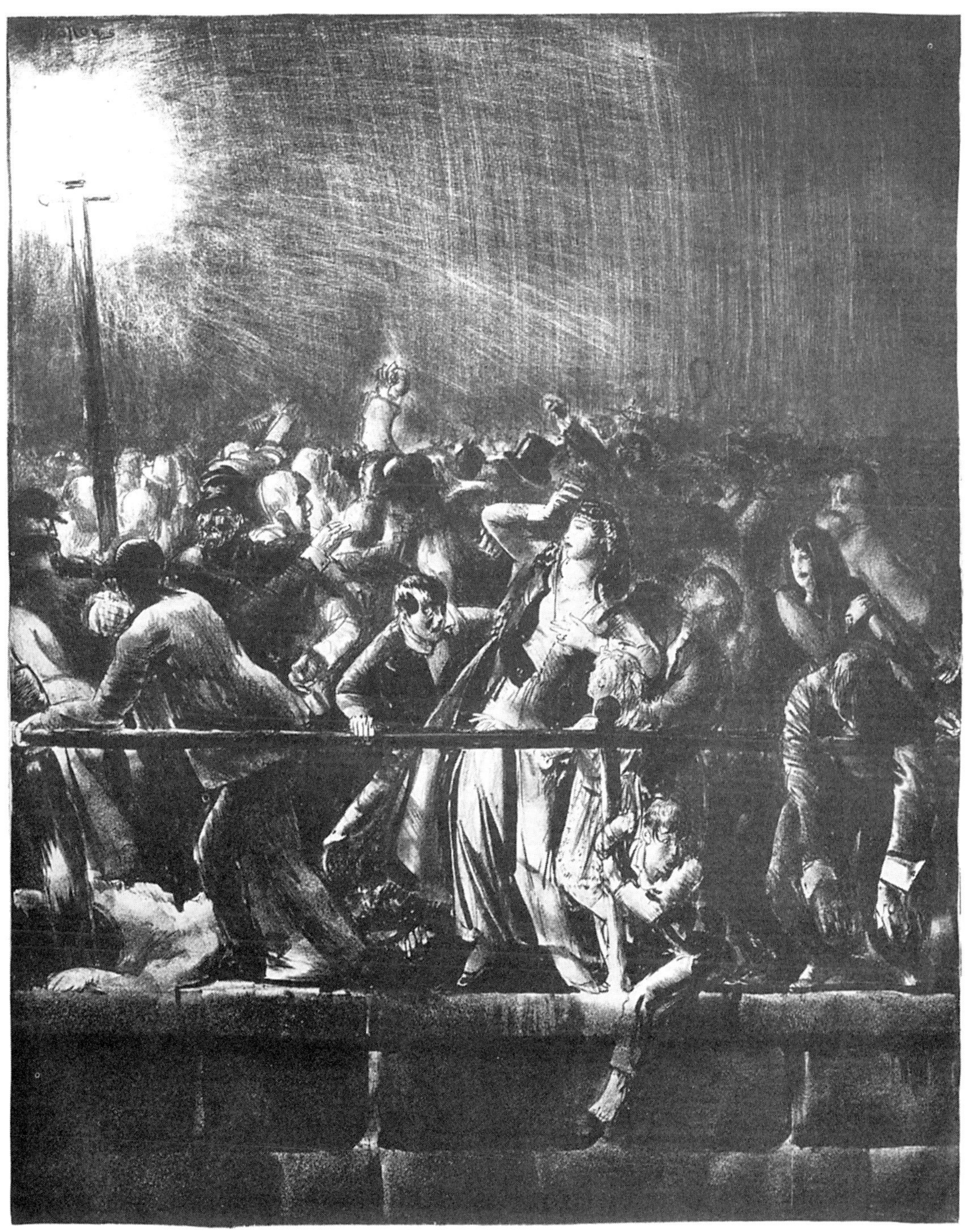

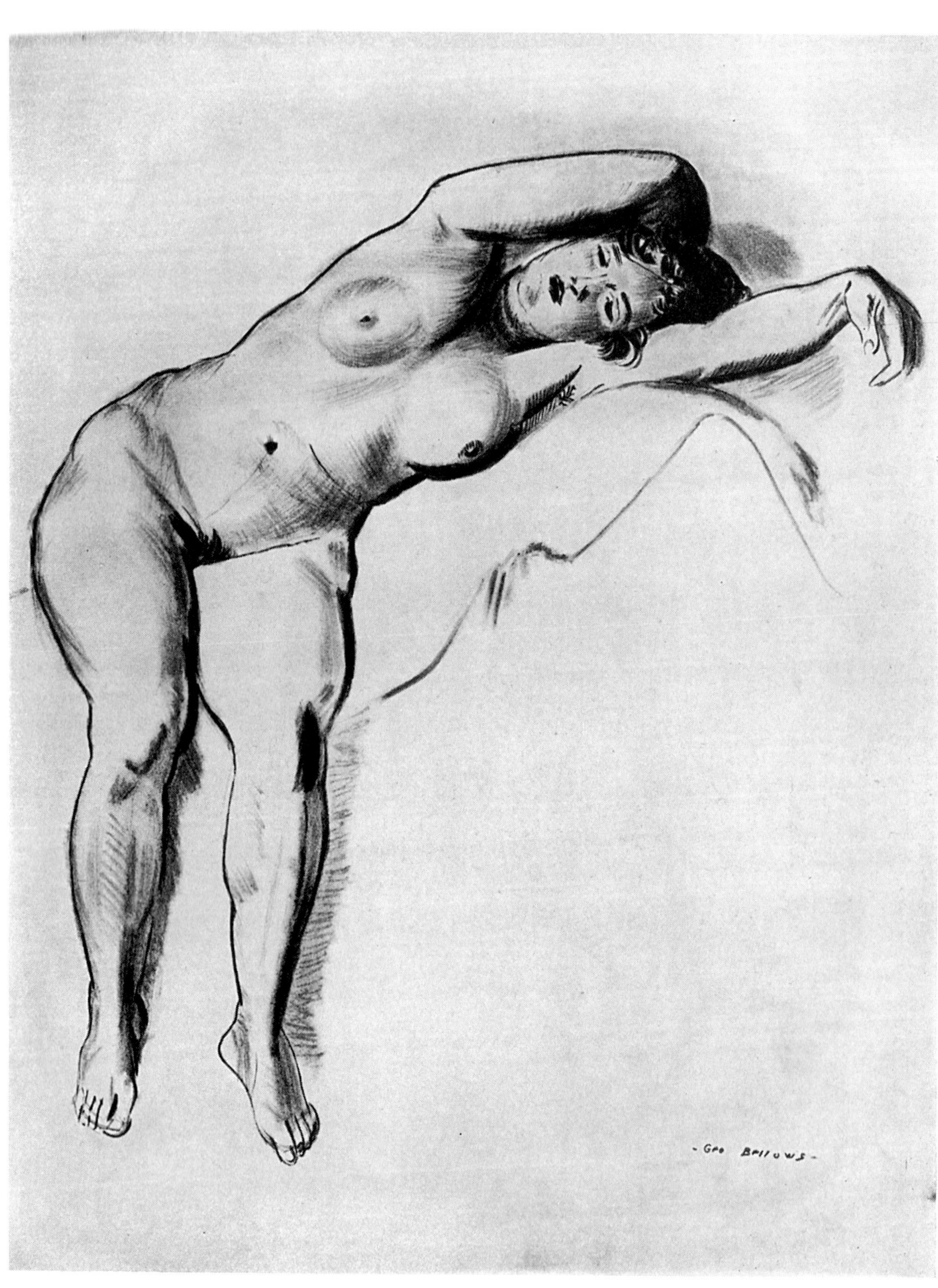

68   *Nude Study, Woman Stretched on Bed*

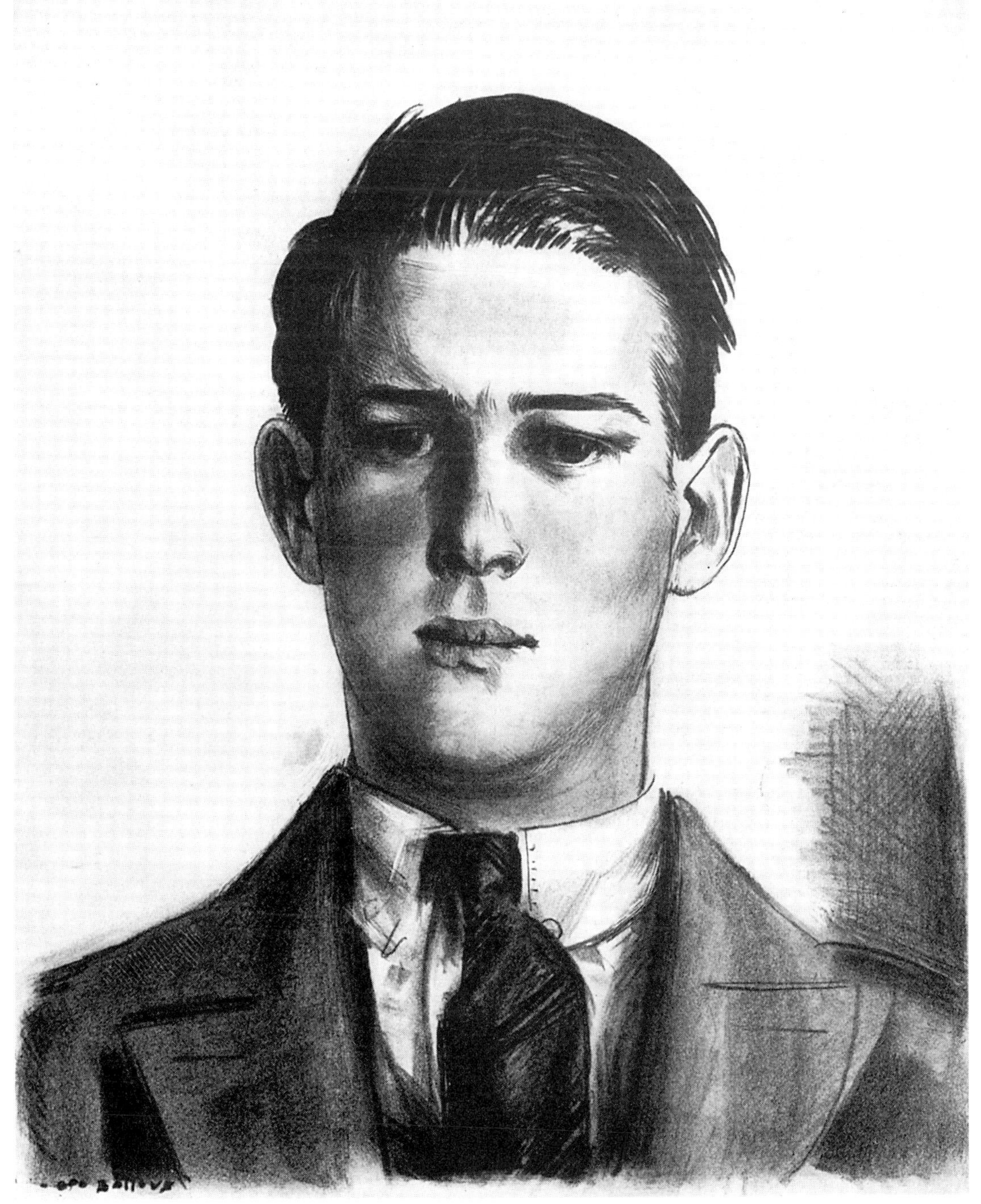

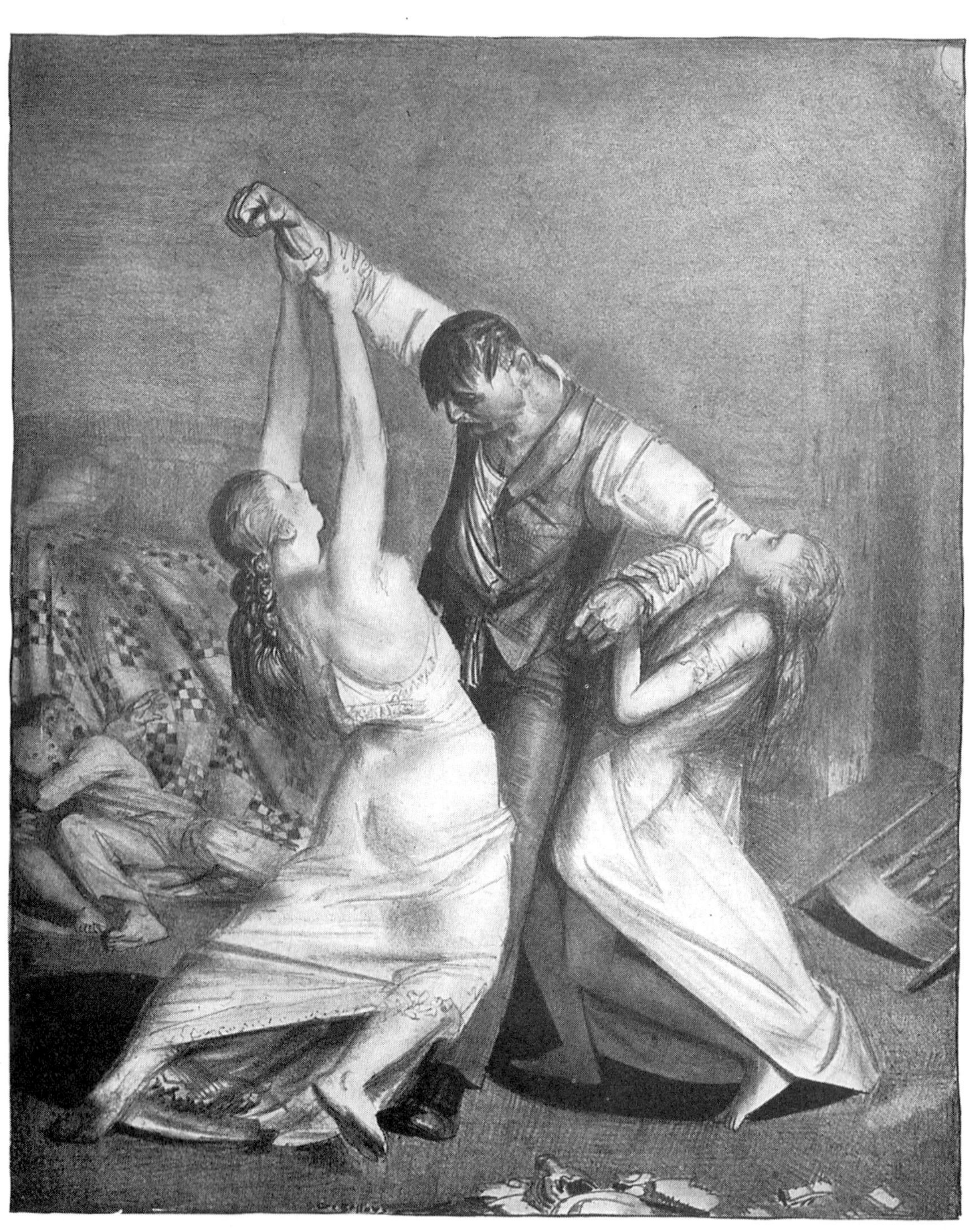

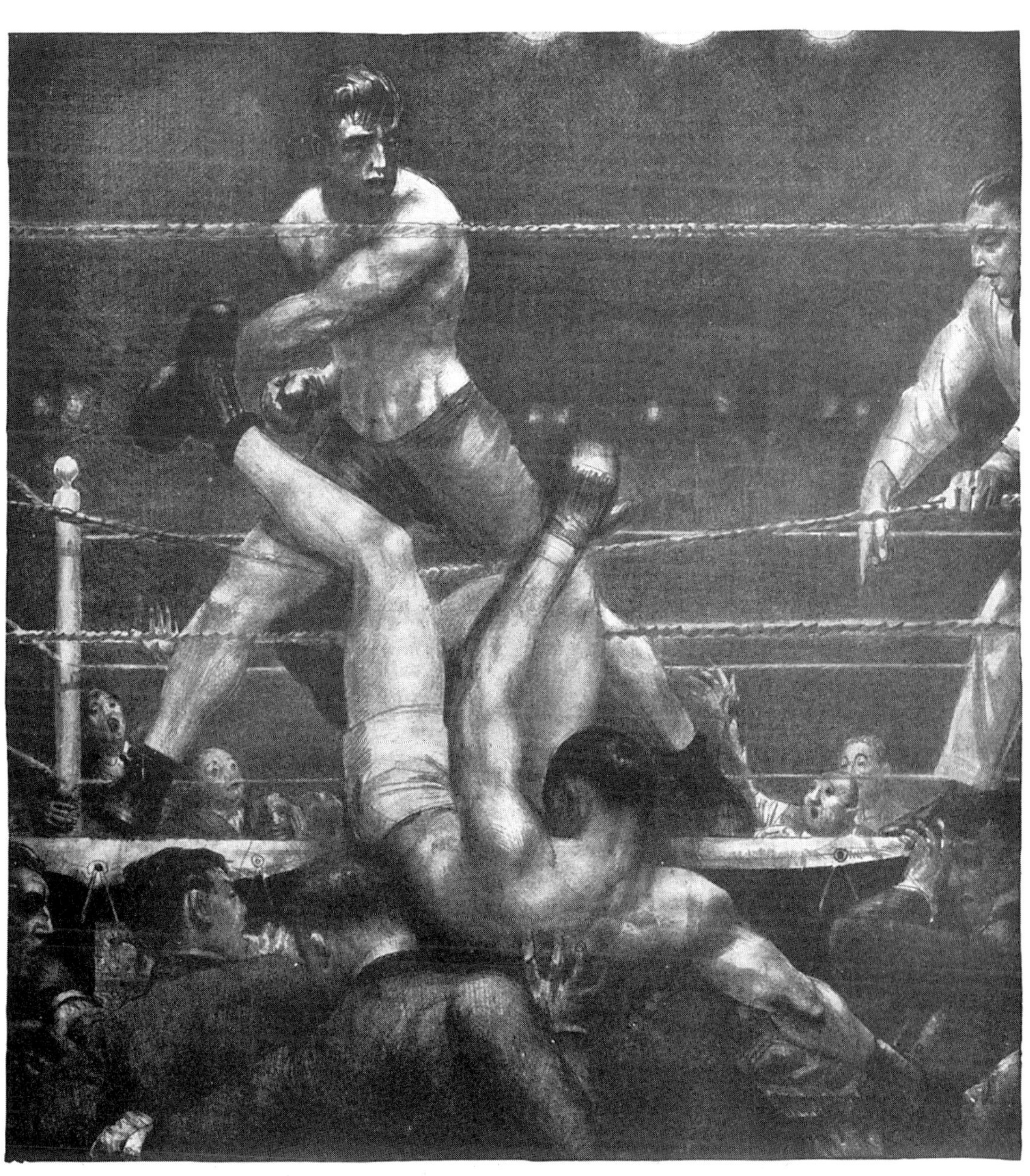

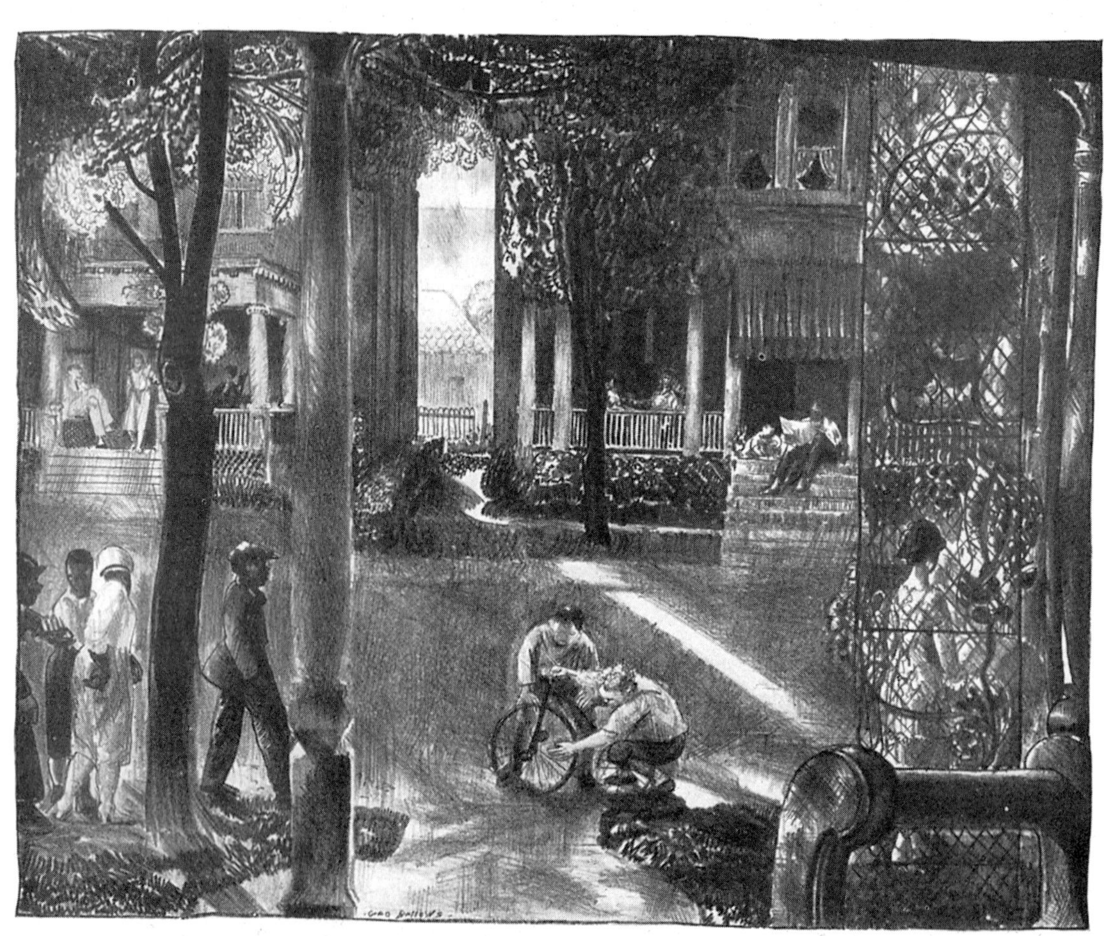

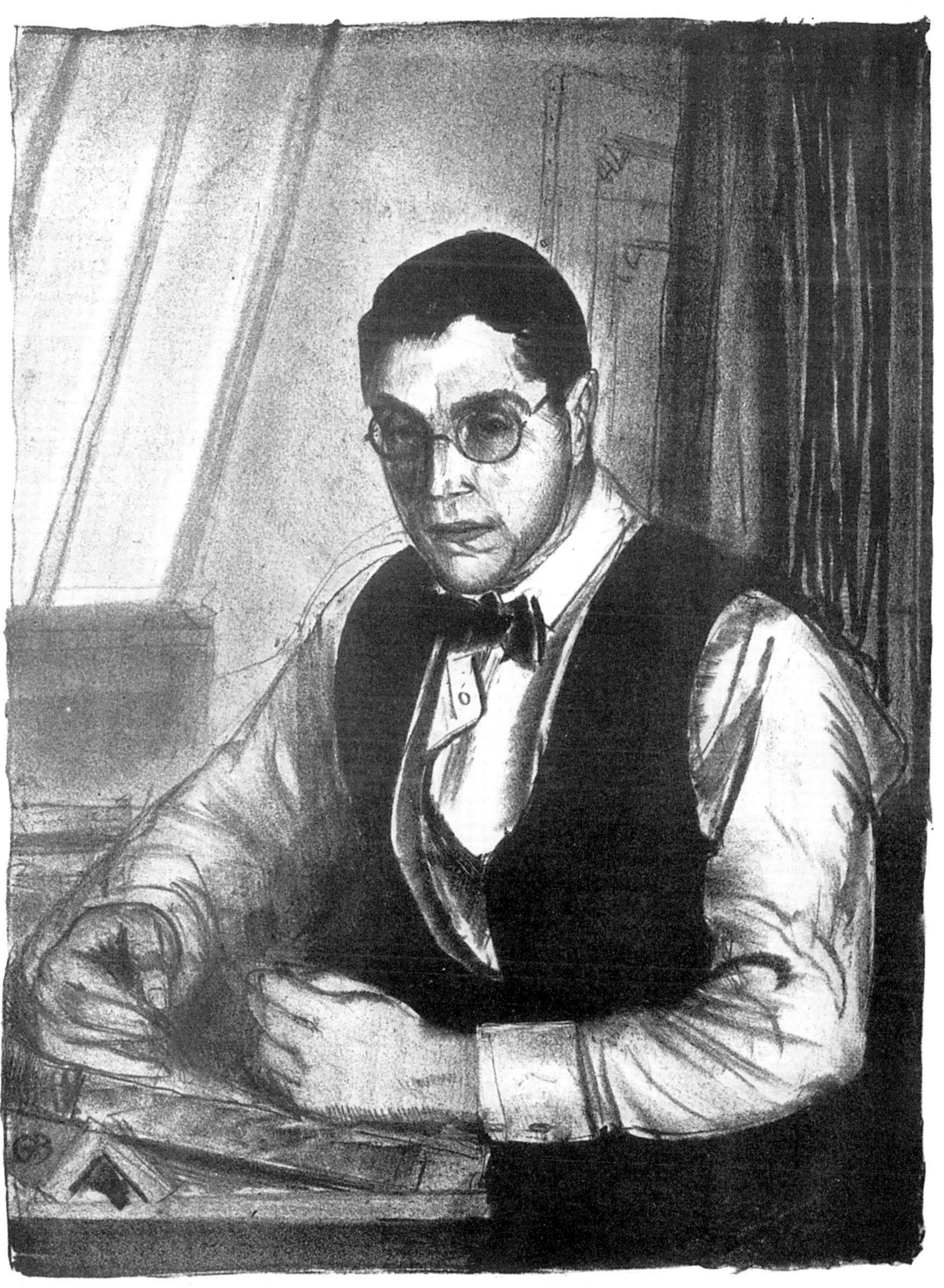

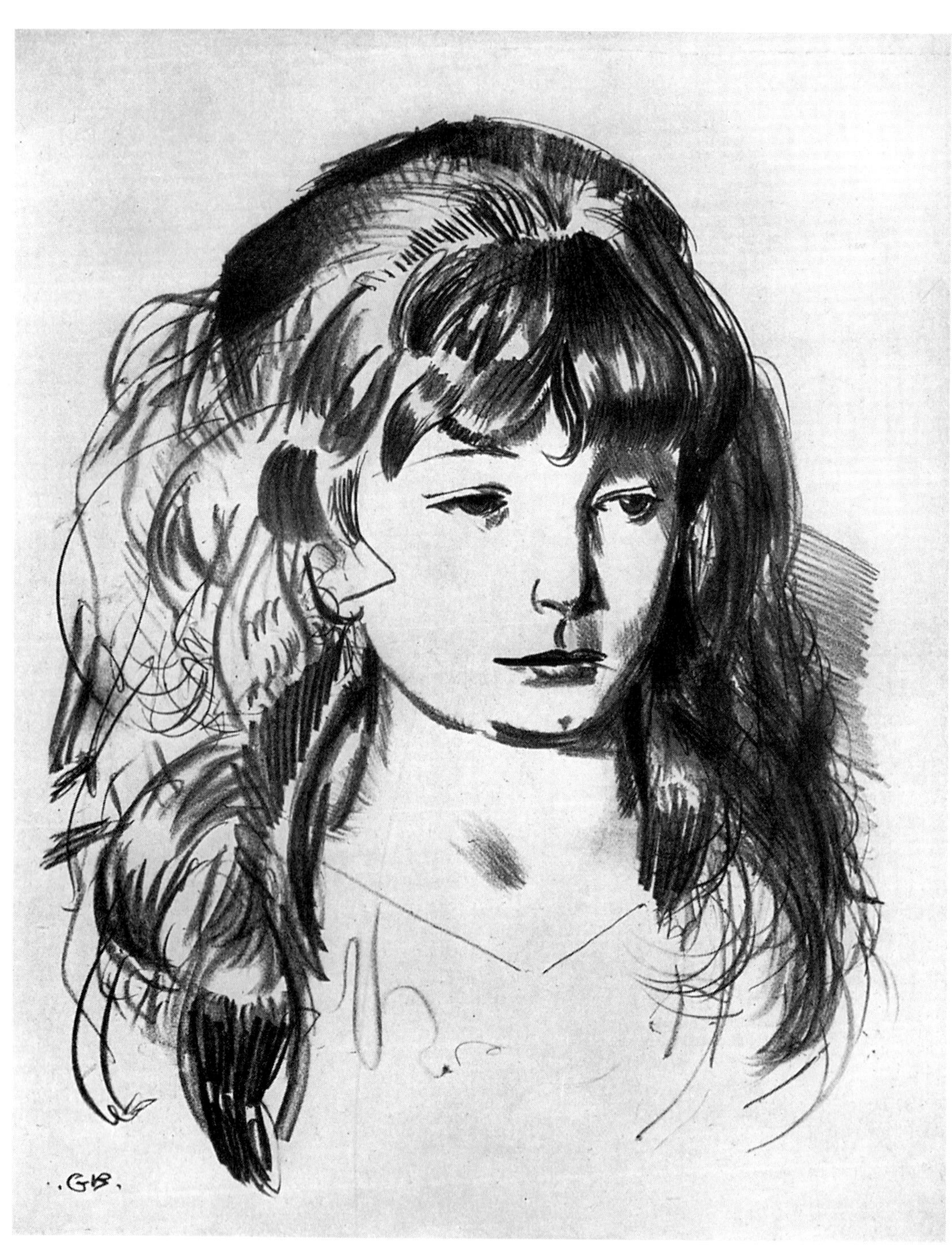

74 *Anne*

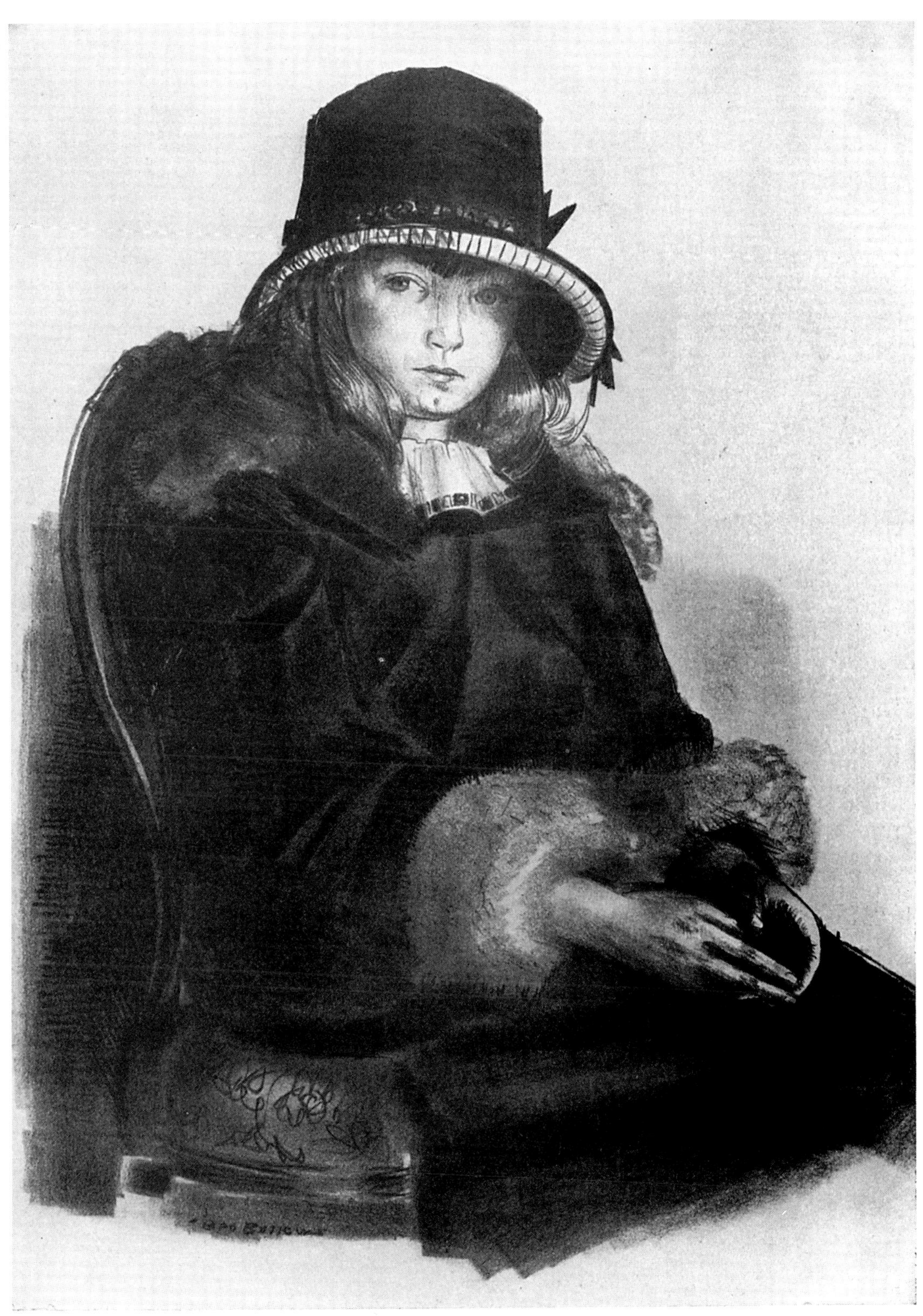

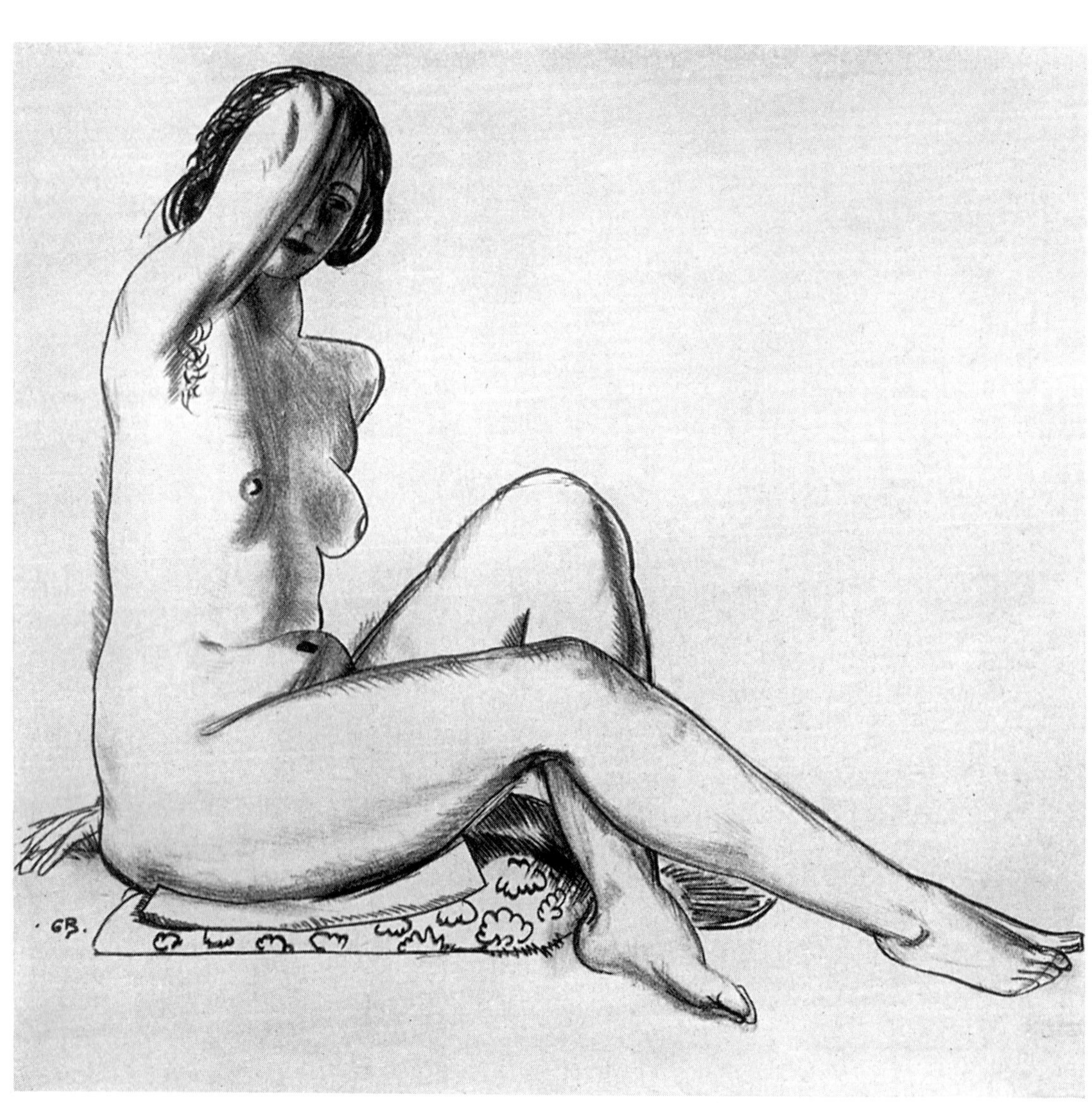

76   *Girl on a Flowered Cushion, Nude*

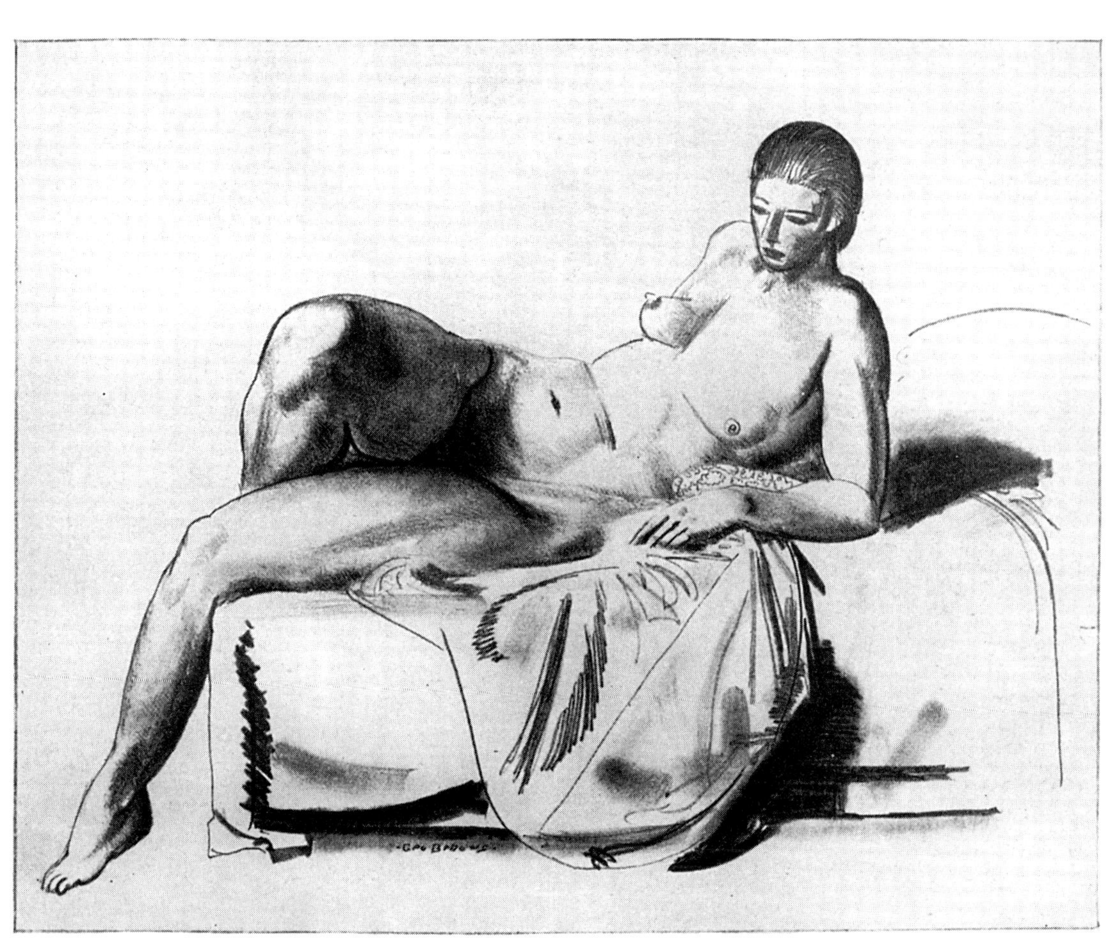

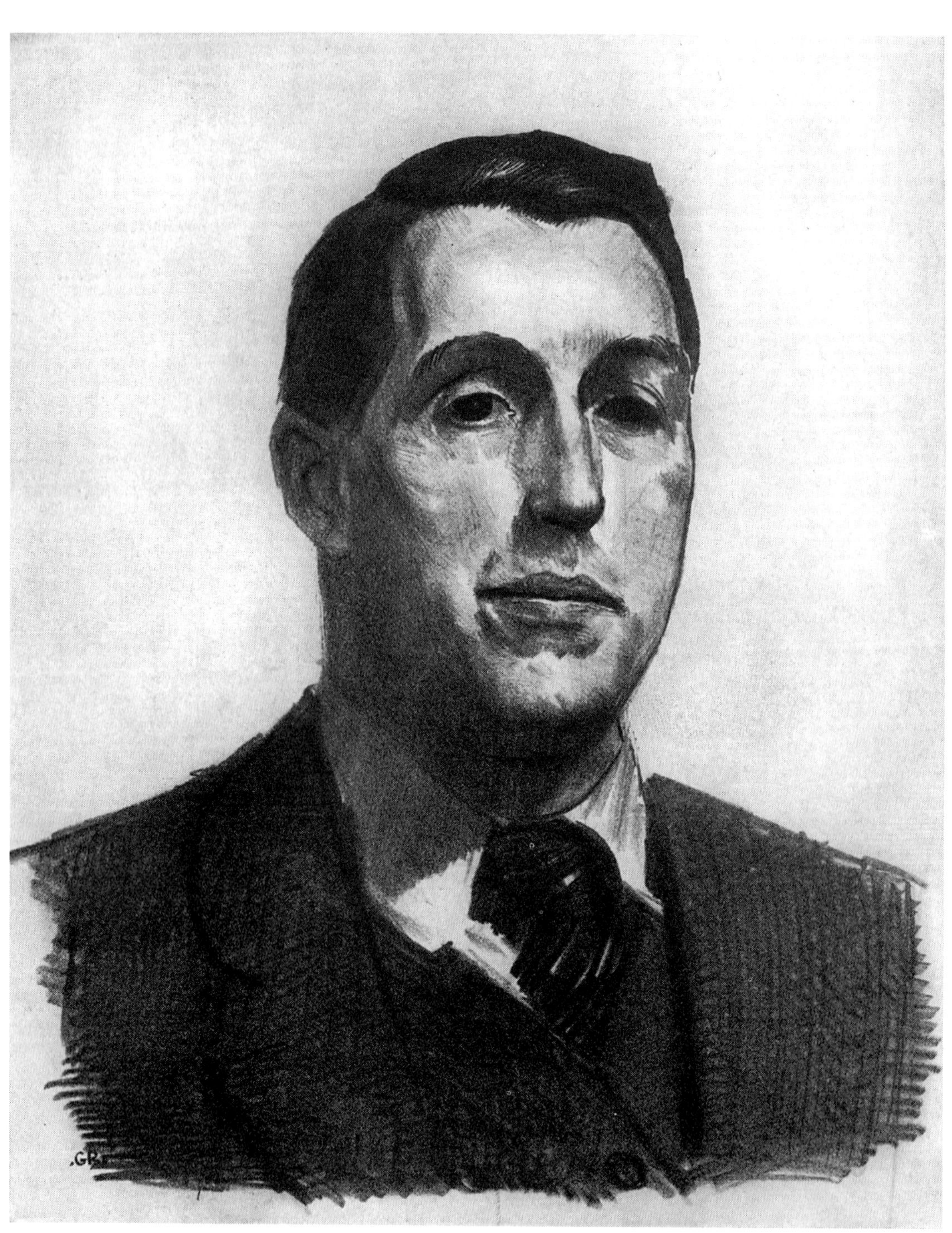

78   *Portrait of Eugene Speicher, No. 2*

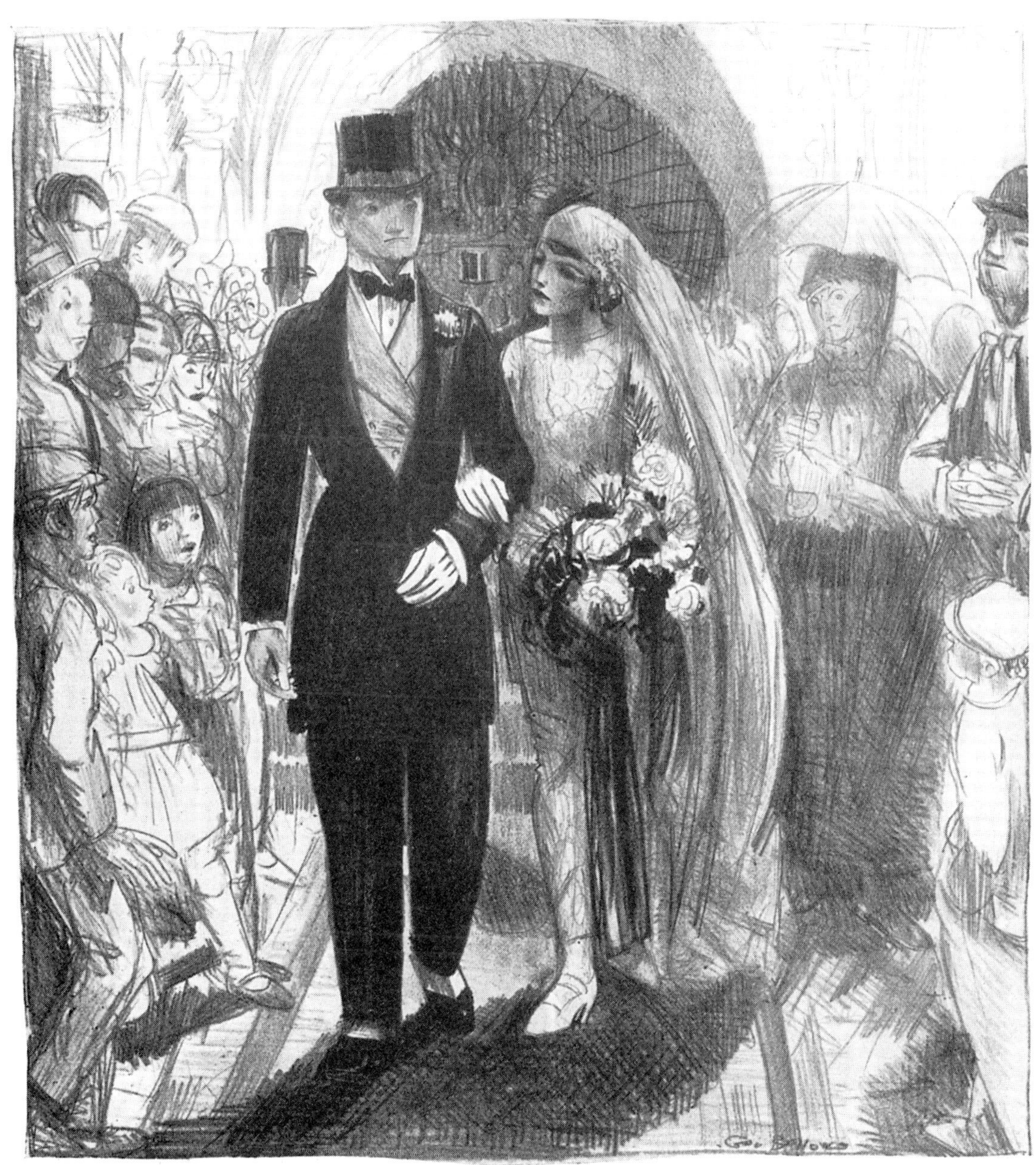

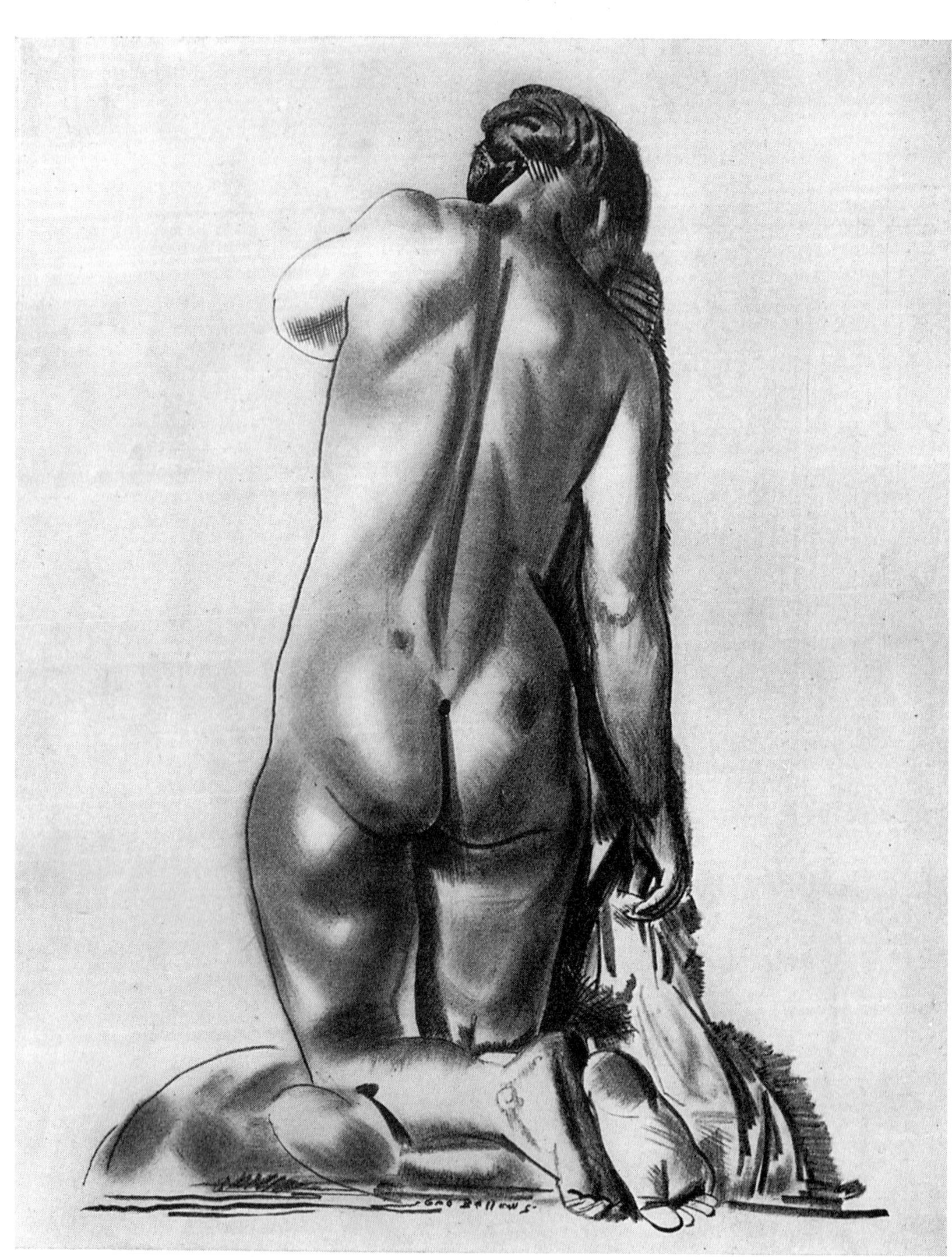

80   *Nude Study, Woman Kneeling on a Pillow*

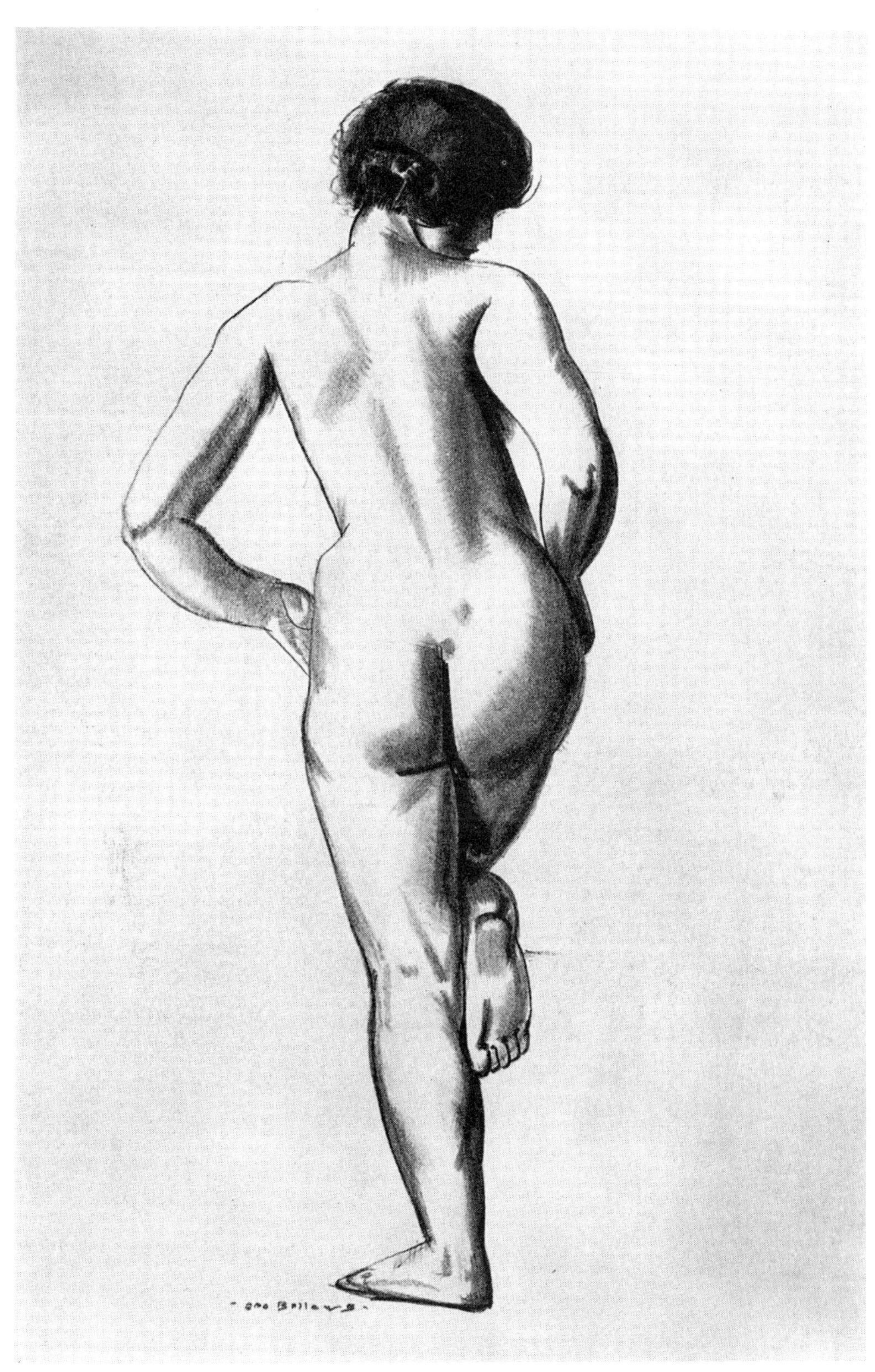

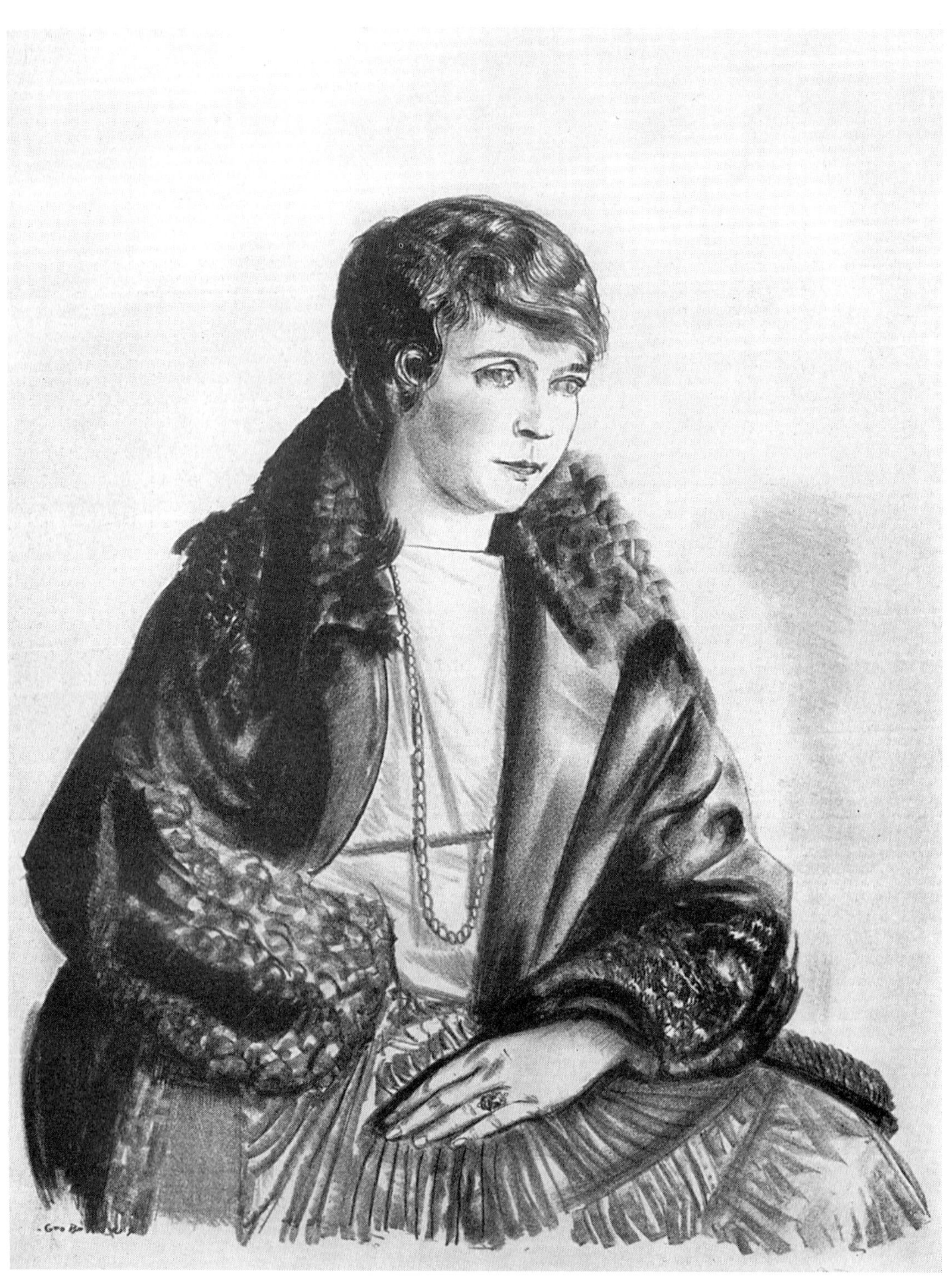

82 *Portrait of Mrs. Herb Roth*

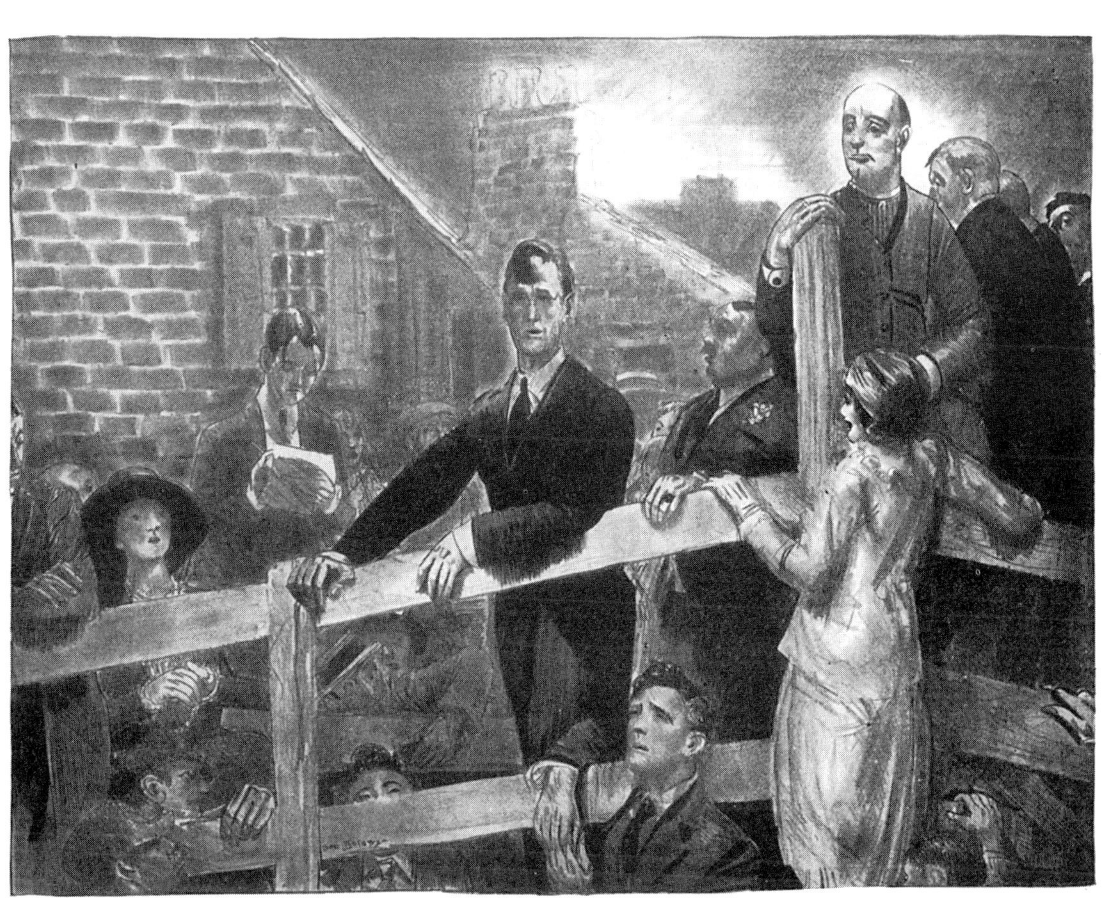

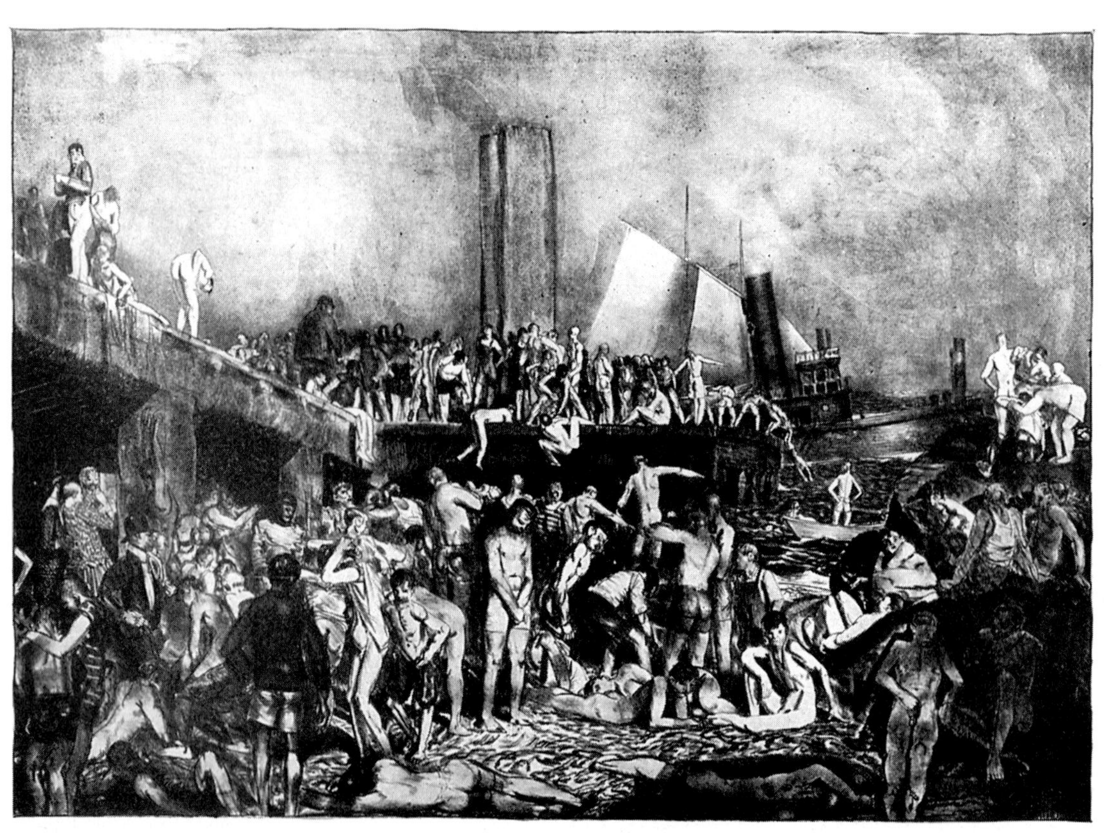

84 *River-front*

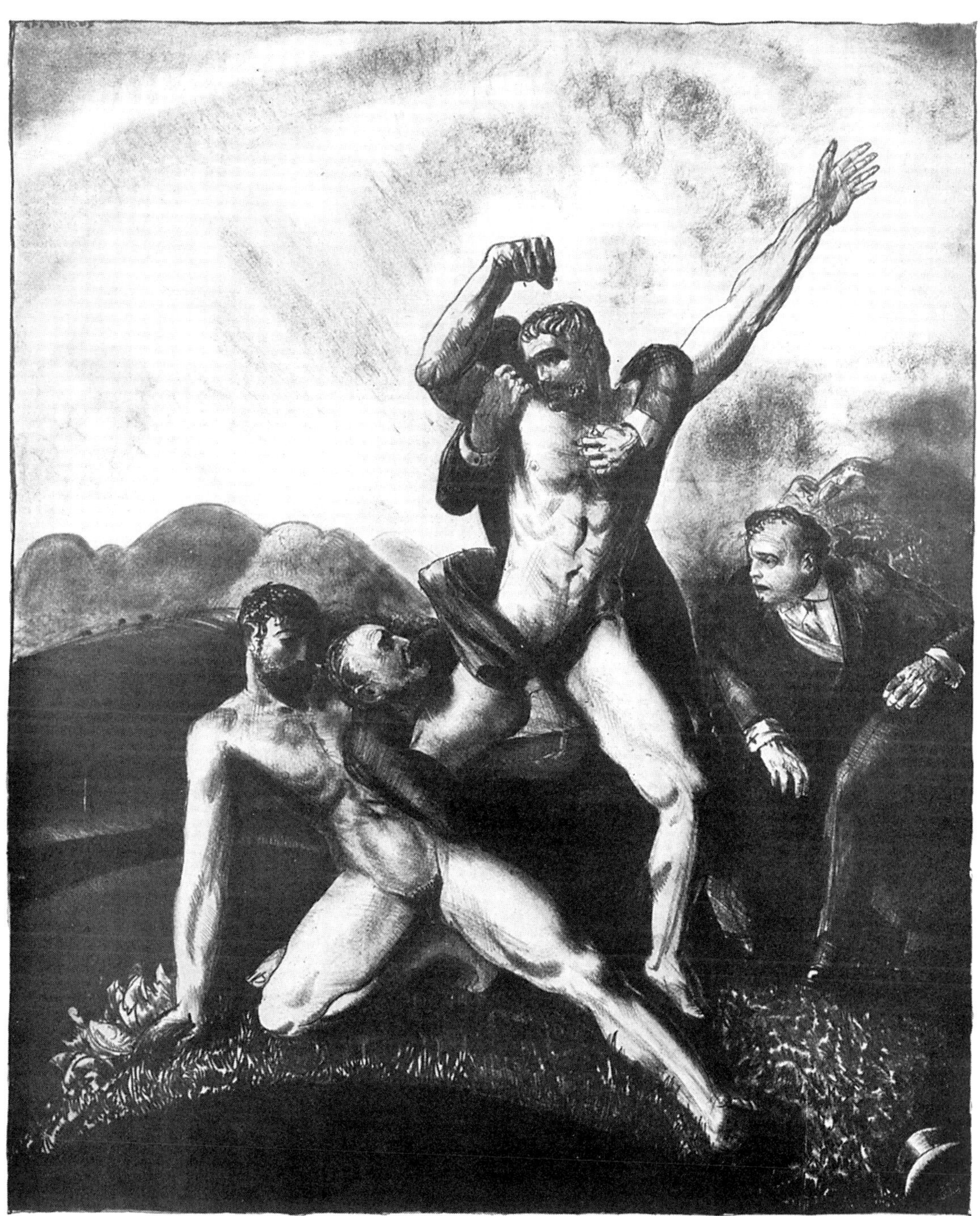

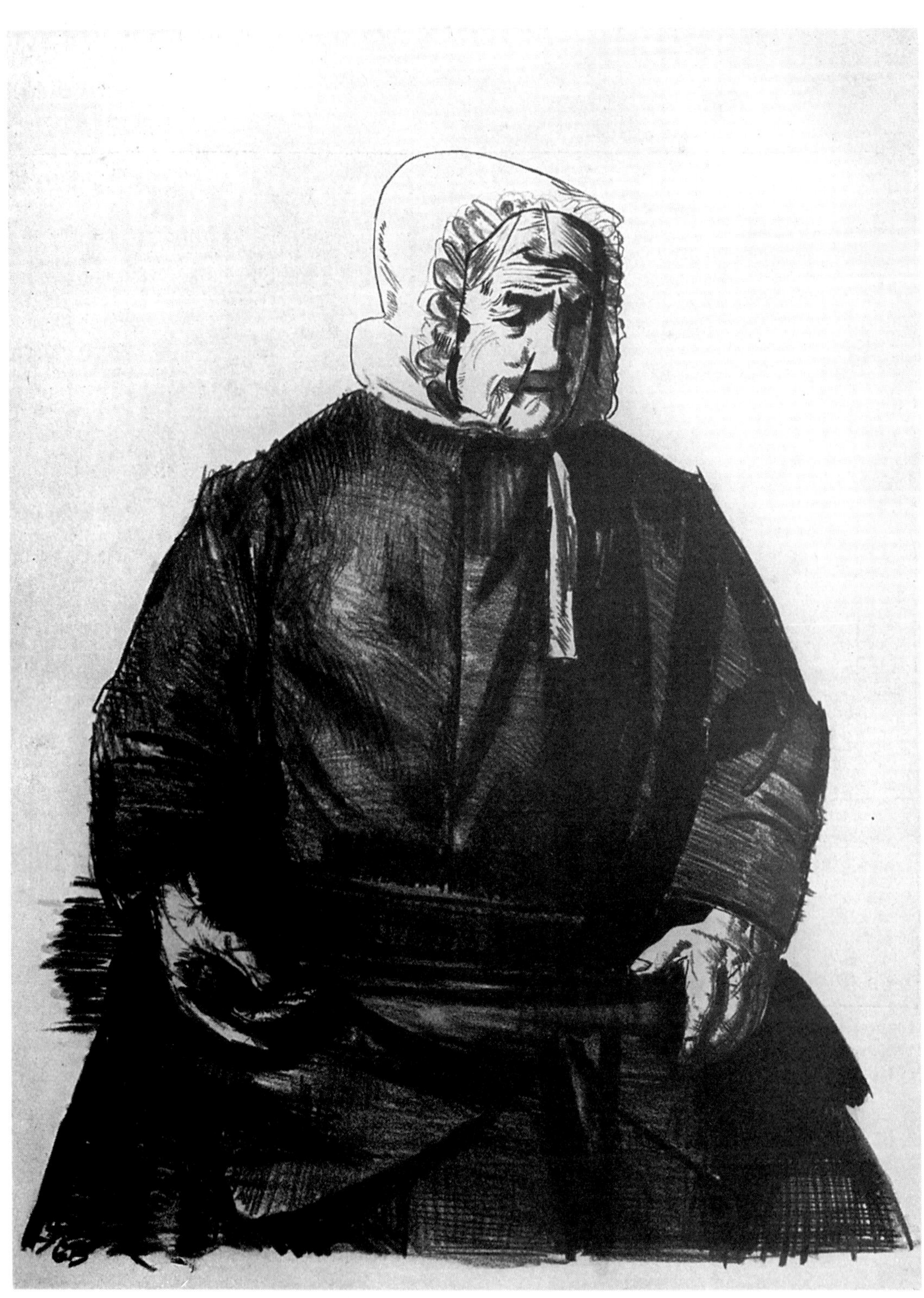

86   *Old Irish Woman*

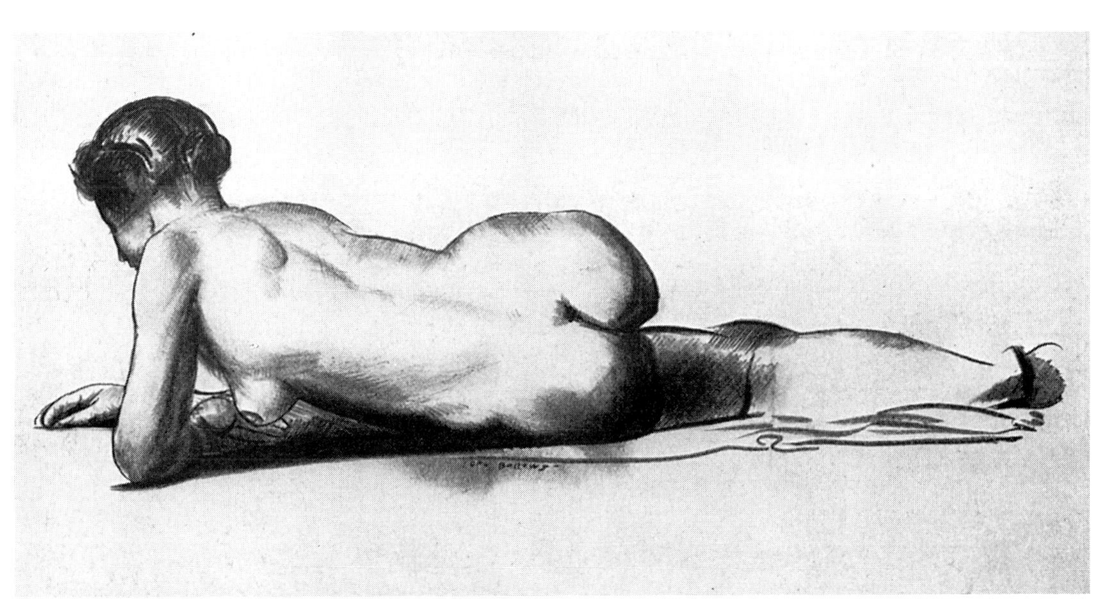